D1296946

Live a Richer Life

A Road Map to Personal Financial Health Following Bankruptcy

©2005 Copyright by the National Foundation for Credit Counseling. All rights reserved.

Live a Richer Life: A Road Map to Personal Financial Health Following Bankruptcy, 2nd Printing, 2007.

No part of this publication may be reproduced, stored in a retrieval system, or transmitted in any form or by any means, graphic, electronic or mechanical, including photocopying, taping, or information storage and retrieval systems, without prior permission of the National Foundation for Credit Counseling.

No portion of this text is in any way intended as legal advice. Readers are strongly advised to consult an attorney regarding specific bankruptcy issues and questions.

Authors

Maryland Council on Economic Education
Mary Ann Hewitt, Executive Director
Amy Rosenkrans, Associate Executive Director
Melissa Groves PhD, Towson University Center Director
Jan Weller, Staff
Stephen Weller, Staff

Technical Consultants
David E. Rice, Esq., Chair, Bankruptcy and Creditors' Rights Law Practice Group, Venable LLP
Professor Michael Staten, Executive Director, Credit Research Center, McDonough School of Business, Georgetown University

Counselor Certification Team
Margo Mitchell, President & CEO, CCCS of Oklahoma, Inc.
Mark R. Munzenberger, Training Manager, GreenPath, Inc./dba GreenPath Debt Solutions
Sara Allen, Executive Director, CCCS of Northern Colorado & Southeast Wyoming
Dawn Lockhart, President, CCCS of Jacksonville (Family Counseling Services)
Kenneth R. King, Executive Director, CCCS of Sheboygan (A Division of Family Service Association)
Denise Surratt, Director of Counseling, CCCS of Greater New Orleans, Inc.

Contributors
CCCS of the Miami Valley (Sponsored By Lutheran Social Services)
CCCS/A Division of Compass of Carolina
CCCS of Greater Dallas, Inc.
CCCS of Western North Carolina, Inc.
Credit Counseling Network dba CCCS of Greater Washington, Inc.
CCCS of Forsyth County, Inc.
CCCS of Northeastern Wisconsin (FISC— Program of Goodwill Industries)
FamilyMeans Consumer Credit Counseling Service
CCCS of Oklahoma, Inc.
CCCS of Central Alabama (Division of Gateway)

Senior Editors
Michael R. Turner, Senior Vice President, Director of Grants, Housing & Stewardship
National Foundation for Credit Counseling
Michael Gelb, Gelb Strategies

Contents

CHAPTER ONE

Rebuilding Following Bankruptcy

What to Expect

You are about to complete the **bankruptcy** process. As you know, your personal financial life has undergone a significant change. On the positive side, you have a fresh financial start. Many, perhaps all, of your debts are about to be **discharged**, and you will no longer be obligated to pay them; your **creditors** should no longer contact you to demand payment of your discharged debts; and your budget will become more manageable. If you have filed a **Chapter 13 bankruptcy,** you are still paying off at least a portion of your old debts, but on a monthly plan that is easy to keep track of and which must be incorporated into your budget planning.

On the other hand, your bankruptcy also has some unpleasant side effects. If you are not already encountering these, you will begin to feel them more fully in the weeks and months ahead. For one thing, you will be asked on any number of different types of documents such as applications for jobs, insurance or loans if you have ever declared bankruptcy. Although it may be unpleasant, you should answer these questions truthfully in every instance. Your bankruptcy is a matter of public record, and a dishonest answer might be considered fraud that could expose you to future legal consequences. Even if fraud is not an issue, you can sour a new employment or business relationship if someone finds out later that you were less than open about it. Your bankruptcy also means you will have a more difficult time obtaining credit,

and you will almost certainly have to pay higher interest rates or accept other unfavorable terms because of your bankruptcy. In addition to these high costs, you are also a prime target for "**predatory lenders**." Predatory lenders often seek out people who are just emerging from bankruptcy. It is, therefore, important that you learn what to look for in considering offers of credit.

But the most important fact about your bankruptcy is that it has given you an opportunity to retake control of your financial life.

As a major first step, we strongly recommend that you follow Rule #1: *Don't even consider borrowing money for any reason until you have reorganized your financial affairs and proven that you can live within a budget.* While carefully planned use of credit will almost certainly be part of your life again, during this interim period new credit and new debts should be off limits. Stop using any credit cards you still have. It also means no car loans, no bank loans, no credit from department stores, and no loans from friends. You will be tempted by many different types of offers almost every day to break this rule, but you must resist these temptations at this stage of your life.

Whatever the reason for your bankruptcy—events beyond your control such as a costly illness or mismanagement of your financial affairs—it is now essential that you take a step back, develop a financial plan and learn to live on a budget. There is a good chance you will have to make significant and permanent changes in your spending habits and overall financial behavior before you can safely take on even a small amount of new debt.

We have created this course with you, the bankruptcy filer, in mind. But the principles and practices discussed in this book are valid for any person who is interested in long-term financial health. Much of what we recommend may not be possible for you right away. Your budget may not allow you to save for your retirement at this time, but as soon as it does, you should begin to save as described in this book. Your ability to buy insurance may be very limited right now. But, as you learn the importance of protecting yourself from the severe financial impact of certain losses, you will likely want to find a way to include the purchase of additional insurance in your budget.

How to Read This Book

This book is intended to help you make the necessary adjustments in your approach to personal money matters. It will provide you with the tools and the knowledge to build a new financial life based on sound financial principles. The goal is to help you reach a true state of financial wellness.

You will get the most out of your reading if you work with your counselor and complete each of the exercises in earnest. The budget analysis is especially important. Even if your financial difficulties were caused by events beyond your control, how you have reacted to those events—in short, your financial behavior—is what brought you to this point. It is **vital** that you and your family understand how and why you made those financial decisions. This does **not** mean they were necessarily bad decisions; it just means you must understand why you made them, what the impact of those decisions was, and what you might have done differently knowing what you will learn in this course. To help you in this process, we have included a glossary in the back of the book to explain terms which might not be familiar to you. Everywhere you see a word in ***bold italics*** like this, refer to the glossary for a better understanding of that word's definition.

CHAPTER TWO

Use the "Economic Way of Thinking" to Choose Between "Wants" and "Needs"

"There is no such thing as a free lunch."

Now, let's begin helping you change your money behavior. The very first step in that process is to encourage you to try a new way to make money choices in your life. We call it the "Economic Way of Thinking."

The "Economic Way of Thinking"

An important economic concept is that nothing in life is free. Every action has costs. Every decision has consequences, some good and some bad. Smart decision-making involves weighing the costs and benefits of the different choices. The economic way of thinking is based on the following principles:

- People cannot have everything they want.
- People must make choices.
- Every choice involves a cost.
- People's choices have consequences.

Personal Decision-Making

The personal resources that an individual uses to satisfy his/her wants include time, money, and talents. Those resources are used to purchase goods and services. But we all know that we cannot have all of the goods and services we want and that we have to make choices. Now that you have filed for bankruptcy, your choices are almost certainly more limited than in the past. In the next few pages, we will walk you though one example to illustrate thoughtful decision-making.

Hit the Road Jack— A Decision-Making Exercise

Jack has just about completed the bankruptcy process. His bankruptcy was the result of a medical emergency that wiped out his savings as he tried to pay for care that wasn't covered by insurance. Even after dipping into savings, Jack still had bills that were too big to pay with his current income. He sought a fresh start through bankruptcy. He *reaffirmed* some of his debt, but much of it is about to be discharged.

Jack's 1989 car has just broken down. His mechanic says that he will be able to repair it for $300. Jack does not have the money on hand to pay for the repair—unless he foregoes some other expenditure that is in his budget. Jack must decide whether to borrow to make the repairs or to temporarily stop using the car. Among the most important issues he must weigh are how and at what cost he can travel the 20 miles to work if he fixes the car or if he doesn't.

Using the Decision-Making Grid, let's evaluate Jack's alternatives.

Decision-Making Grid

Option	Cost	Convenience	Safety	No Debt	Totals
1. Fix Car	2	10	8	0	20
2. Public transportation	7	5	3	8	23
3. Carpool	9	4	9	10	33
4. Buy car	0	8	8	0	16

Step #1: Define the problem.

Jack needs transportation to his job which is 20 miles from his home. He must decide whether to fix his car or find other means of transportation.

Step #2: List all the alternatives and possible solutions.

Jack has identified four possible solutions to his problem:

1. He can pay the $300 to fix his car. That would disrupt his budget plan, but he prefers the freedom and reliability of driving to work each day.
2. Jack could choose to use public transportation. The local bus stop is only a half mile from his house, and it drops him off near work, but it runs through a high-crime neighborhood. Also, city busses are not very reliable. The last time he took the bus to work, he was two hours late.
3. Jack has a friend who works the same hours as he does who might be willing to carpool if Jack shares the gas expense. This also will enable the friend to use the High Occupancy Vehicle lanes when he drives to work, thereby reducing the commute time.
4. Jack could buy a new car. This option violates rule #1 from the first chapter—**do not borrow money at this stage in your life.** Jack very likely cannot pay cash. The loan he might get for such a purchase, while appearing manageable, will probably have a very high interest rate and very severe penalties for late payments.

Step #3: Identify important factors to evaluate alternatives/choices.

Certain considerations will be important to Jack as he makes his decision. Jack alone can determine how important these factors are. Every individual has different criteria, which is why a "want" for one person might be a "need" for someone else. Jack's most important factors affecting his decision are:

*   Cost
*   Personal convenience
*   Safety
*   Avoiding debt

Step #4: Evaluate the alternatives/choices.

Jack must now assign a weight to each factor in order to evaluate his alternatives. Using a Decision-Making Grid like the one above, he will use a scale of 1-10 to weigh each factor in terms of its benefit, with 10 being the most beneficial.

Using the information in this Decision-Making Grid, Jack can make his decision on the basis of careful evaluation, not impulse.

What choice do you recommend for Jack? The choice with the highest ranking is the most reasoned, rational choice for *Jack* based upon his personal situation—which includes having filed for bankruptcy. Jack would very much like to buy a new car, but his financial circumstances have temporarily made that a very bad choice—in fact, the worst choice of the four. Someone else with a different set of priorities or in a different personal situation might have made a different decision. But for Jack, based upon the factors that are important to him, carpooling makes the most sense. It is not especially convenient for him, but he understands that he will have to change his behavior to avoid going into debt again.

Step #5: Make a decision.

Jack talked to his friend, explained his predicament, and asked if they could work out a carpool arrangement for at least a few weeks. Jack can now save part of the gas money he would normally spend each week and use it to eventually get his car repaired, which he considers much more convenient.

Your Personal Decision-Making Exercise

The same Decision-Making Grid can be used for your own personal decisions. Identify a problem that you must address. Follow the five steps and evaluate the costs and benefits of your alternatives using the Decision-Making Grid in the appendix.

CHAPTER THREE

Developing Sound Financial Habits

This chapter will help you analyze your current thinking about money and introduce sound money management habits that are critical to long-term financial health. Again, some of what we suggest is not possible right now as a result of your bankruptcy. However, by learning to budget and by developing these habits, you will soon have extra money available each month to expand your options. Right now, your financial horizon is very short—you may be focused on making it to the end of the week or month on your paycheck. As you develop these habits, however, your horizon will begin to expand. You will soon see your savings grow and future financial goals become a real possibility. Following is a list of things you want to know or do as you begin to reorder your financial life. Some of them are big things, some are small things, but they all help establish the habits that will enable you to take charge of your money.

Understand how you handle money now.

As a first step back to financial health, you need to take stock. Think long and hard about the choices you have made in the past as you traveled the path to bankruptcy and the choices you must make now as you move forward. You need to be honest with yourself.

If you are a person who has a hard time denying yourself something you want—like the latest electronic gadget or the most expensive new athletic shoes—you need to find a way to remove the temptation. That might mean giving up the credit cards that appear to make things easy to buy. Or, if you can't control an ATM habit, you might need to get rid of your ATM card.

On the other hand, you may be responsible in these areas but have had setbacks because of a job loss or health problems. In that case, you still need to work out a strategy to bounce back. A nationally certified credit counselor can help by acting as your financial "coach." The good ones cost very little. In fact, the best ones will help you even if you can't afford to pay them.

To help with your self-assessment of your attitude about money, read each of the topics below and choose the answer, or any combination of answers, that you believe represents the best financial habit or habits. If you have other ideas, write your own choice in the blank slot.

_____ 1. **Spending:**
   A. You know where your money is being spent.
   B. You know where most of your money is being spent.
   C. You have no idea where your money is going.
   D.

_____ 2. **Credit cards (assume you will eventually have credit cards):**
   A. You should not use credit cards.
   B. You should be able to pay off all of your credit card bills each month.
   C. If you can't pay them off, you should pay more than the minimum amount due each month.
   D. You need only pay the minimum amount due each month.
   E. Transferring balances to delay payments is okay.
   F.

_____ 3. **Credit cards:**
   A. You should have as many cards as you want. Many cards mean you can afford to have them.
   B. You should have no more than two or three cards of any kind.
   C. Department store cards and bank cards are the same thing.
   D. You can have many cards as long as you pay them all off each month.
   E.

_____ 4. **Credit cards:**
   A. You should always make your payments by the due date.
   B. It is okay if your payments are sometimes late because of your pay cycle.
   C. Your interest rate will stay the same whether your payment is late or not.
   D. Late payment penalties are not that bad.
   E.

_____ 5. **Housing:**
   A. Owning a home is better than renting.
   B. Renting is better than owning a home.
   C. Your rent or house payment should not be more than 30 percent of your take-home pay.
   D. Sharing rent with a roommate is a sign of failure.
   E.

_____ 6. **Savings:**
   A. It is okay to use savings for day-to-day living expenses.
   C. It is okay to use savings to pay monthly bills.
   D. You should have 1-3 months of living expenses saved.
   E. You should have 3-6 months of living expenses saved.
   F. Savings are a nice thing to have, unless you can't afford to save.
   G.

_____ 7. **Savings:**
   A. You should keep your savings at home.
   B. You should keep your savings in your checking account.
   C. You should keep your savings in a savings account at a bank or credit union.
   D. You should keep your savings in a money market account or fund.
   E. You should keep your savings in 6 or 12 month certificates of deposit (CDs).
   F. You should keep your savings in U.S. Government savings bonds.
   G.

_____ 8. **Transportation:**
   A. You drive your car until it no longer runs.
   B. You buy a new car, SUV, or truck every few years.
   C. You lease your vehicles.
   D. You rely on public transportation.
   E. You carpool.
   F.

_____ 9. **Transportation:**
   A. You like to pay cash for vehicles.
   B. You should make a down payment of 20-50 percent of the cost of the vehicle.
   C. You should make a down payment of less than 20 percent of the cost of the vehicle.
   D. Making a down payment is not important.
   E.

_____ 10. **Transportation:**
   A. You should finance a vehicle for 6 to 8 years.
   B. You should finance a vehicle for 4 or 5 years.
   C. You should finance a vehicle for 2 or 3 years.
   D. You should lease a vehicle rather than buy.
   E.

_____ 11. **Vacation:**
   A. You like to vacation by relaxing at home.
   B. You like to vacation at the beach or in the mountains.
   C. You like to vacation by traveling and staying in hotels.
   D. You like to vacation by camping.
   E. You like to vacation by visiting family.
   F.

_____ 12. **Vacation:**
   A. You should pay for vacation by saving money in advance.
   B. You should pay for vacation by charging the amount on credit cards, as long as you pay them off the following month.
   C. You should pay for vacation by using credit cards and start a six-month payoff plan for yourself. Otherwise, you will never go on vacation.
   D.

_____ 13. **Retirement:**
   A. You have a job-related retirement plan, but you can't afford to contribute.
   B. You have a job-related retirement plan, but you can make better investment decisions on your own.
   C. Your retirement will be Social Security.
   D. You should take full advantage of a job-related retirement plan because earnings are tax-deferred.
   E.

_____ 14. **Retirement accounts:**
   A. You should put 5 percent of your yearly income into retirement accounts.
   B. You should put 5-10 percent of your yearly income into retirement accounts.
   C. You should put 10-15 percent of your yearly income into retirement accounts.
   D. You should put more than 15 percent of your yearly income into retirement accounts.
   E. You should put nothing into a retirement account; you plan to be rich or dead by then.
   F.

_____ 15. **Retirement accounts:**
   A. You prefer Certificates of Deposit (CDs).
   B. You prefer just the stock of the company you work for.
   C. You prefer stocks of several companies.
   D. You prefer mutual funds.
   E. You prefer investing in real estate.
   F. You prefer buying U.S. Savings bonds.
   G.

You should discuss the answers to these questions with your credit counselor or in class. The following answers, however, generally reflect sound financial habits:

1. A
2. A, B, or C
3. B
4. A
5. A or B, and C
6. E
7. C or D. You need to have easy access to savings for emergencies.
8. All are okay.
9. A or B
10. B, C, or D are okay. You should not finance a vehicle for longer than five years.
11. All are okay.
12. A or B
13. D
14. A, B, C, or D
15. All are okay; however, savings accounts will not keep up with inflation. Generally, mutual funds will beat inflation over the long term, and real estate can be a very good investment for the long term. But all investments involve some risks that you need to understand when deciding how to invest. Talk with a financial advisor to decide what's best for you.

Developing Good Financial Habits

Calculate your income precisely.

To create a reliable budget, you need to know exactly how much income you can count on. You need to be realistic and count only what you are earning right now. Future income, from any source, may or may not be there in the end. A change in business conditions, for example, may postpone that raise you've been expecting, so you shouldn't count on it in your planning until it shows up in your paycheck.

Spend Wisely.

Purchases that maintain or increase their value and that are paid for are assets. Assets help to build wealth. That means owning a home usually helps build wealth (although it will take many years before it is fully paid for). Savings and investments that increase in value over time also help to build wealth. Although we certainly need clothes, they don't help to build wealth. When you use a credit card to purchase an item, you are borrowing money. You have to decide whether it is a good idea to borrow money for something that wears out or does not add to your long-term wealth. In other words, do you still want to be paying for items you bought on credit long after they've worn out? And, even when acquiring assets that contribute to your wealth, using credit may stretch your budget or involve interest costs that offset the value of the asset you've acquired.

Pay yourself first.

Believe it or not, the first person you should pay from every paycheck is yourself. This is true even if you are self-employed. Surprised? To reach many of the goals you have set for yourself, you'll need money. If you want to take a nice vacation, buy a house, or enjoy a fairly comfortable retirement, you'll need to save.

Of course, this rule only applies if your income exceeds your expenses each month and leaves you some money to save. This may not be possible right now, but it should be one of your most important goals as you regain your financial footing. As soon as your income exceeds your expenses, you should begin putting some of the extra income into a separate, interest-bearing savings account designed for emergencies. Once you have saved an amount equal to 3-6 months of your take-home (net) income, you should start investing extra income in an investment account that has the potential to grow more rapidly than savings.

Your savings is the safety net that can help keep you from going back into debt. Set up a savings account at your bank or, if one is available, join the credit union where you work and arrange to have the money automatically deducted from your paycheck. This way, the money goes straight into your savings before you are tempted to spend it. You don't have to write a check or go to your bank. If you are self-employed, you should place money into savings or an investment account monthly. Also, don't defeat yourself by withdrawing money from this account before the next deposit.

You should have ready access to this account so that you can use it when emergencies arise. But it should be separate from the account you use to pay regular monthly expenses so that you don't think about it often and are less likely to use it for routine expenses. If you are lucky and don't need to touch it, you will soon have a sizeable nest egg. But, when an emergency arises, you will be better prepared to pay for it. Think how good you will feel the first time you can pay for an unexpected expense without worrying about it or borrowing money.

Bank your raise.

This is an extension of your commitment to "pay yourself first." Since you were able to live on your original budget before your raise or income increase, you should be able to save and invest at least a portion of the increased income. You might also use the new money to speed up the repayment of any debts that were reaffirmed as part of your bankruptcy.

Or, if your budget has been a bit too tight, you might use half of your income increase to improve your quality of life and save the other half. One thing's for sure—don't spend it all. If you do, you will be running in place—no better off financially than before you received the raise.

Prepare to pay periodic expenses that arise regularly a few times a year.

We all have expenses that occur several times a year—car insurance, life insurance, homeowners' and renters' insurance, quarterly tax payments for the self-employed, sewer and water bills, newspaper and magazine subscriptions, tuition, and other taxes such as personal property and real estate taxes. List which of these expenses you have. Add up the amount you need for the entire year and then divide it by 12 months. That is the amount you must put aside each month for these items. Keep this money separate from your checking account. Keep it in a savings account (you could combine this money with your emergency fund). Then you'll know you have the money when you need it.

Take "pre-paid" vacations.

Did you charge your last vacation? Was that a factor in your bankruptcy? Luxury vacations are fun—but not if you don't have the money to pay for them. From now on, it may be better to save for your vacation in advance and pay as you go. It is not that hard to do — providing you make a plan and stick to it.

You could make your vacation one of the periodic expenses and save a little each month. Decide how much you want to spend on your entire vacation. Divide that number by 12 months and put that amount away each month. You could even have the amount deducted from your paycheck each week and funnel it straight into a bank or credit union savings account. That means it could earn interest over the course of the year as you are saving.

If you receive a regular paycheck every two weeks, you will get an "extra" paycheck some months that you can put aside for vacation. If you are paid every two weeks, you receive a paycheck 26 times each year. If you set up your budget based on two paychecks per month – or 24 paychecks a year – getting paid every two weeks is almost like two extra paychecks a year. Why not treat the two extra paychecks a year as a bonus? Use part of them to fund your vacation. Just be sure to put the extra paychecks into a savings account instead of spending them.

Have a gift buying plan.

You can plan for gift-giving just like you plan for vacation. Identify in advance the holidays or birthdays for which you'll give gifts and start setting the money aside as the year goes along. Now that you've experienced bankruptcy, you can see why it is good to pay with cash, a check, or a debit card for the gifts you give. That's an excellent habit to develop. Some banks still offer some form of a "Holiday Club" account. You could decide to join one of those. You would need to be certain to deposit or transfer a specific amount into the account each week or month.

Another way to do this would be to set up your own account or to include "gifts" in your periodic expenses account. You could draw from it throughout the year for birthdays, Mother's Day, Father's Day, and so on. You need to decide how much you will be spending on gifts throughout the year. To do this you need to know yourself and be realistic. Decide on the amount, divide it by 12, and set that amount aside each month. That way, when you give a gift, you can have a bigger smile because you know it's already paid for.

Leave some fun in your budget.

Your budget plan should include some money for fun because without some fun in your budget, you probably won't be able to stick to it. Of course, the fun must be reasonably priced. You may be a professional sports fan, a hobbyist, or a member of a social club. These can be too costly if you pursue them all the time. Indulging once in a while can be okay, if you plan for it. Or, since you're now recovering from your bankruptcy, you may want to find some less pricey things to do for a while. Visit museums, explore what your community has to offer, ride a bicycle or look for free concerts. If you like to watch sports, go to a high school or

college game instead of the pros. Who knows…it could open up a whole new area of entertainment for you! But looking for relatively inexpensive fun is a financial skill you ought to learn.

Plan and save for retirement.

Saving for retirement or college may be hard to handle right after bankruptcy, but they should be among your long-term goals.

It's good to think well in advance about how you will fund your retirement and when you want to retire. Consider whether you want to stop working completely or take on part-time work in your later years. Your ability to have the retirement you want depends on your financial behavior while you're working. There are many retirement savings and investment choices.

First of all, let's consider everyone's safety net— Social Security. Social Security was created as a pay-as-you-go system. That means that current workers are really paying for Social Security for current retirees. A little understood fact about Social Security is that it was never intended to cover all of your retirement needs. It is intended to supplement your other savings and perhaps a company or union pension or your self-employment retirement program. Every year, you should receive a statement from the U.S. Social Security Administration containing information about the amounts you have paid into the fund (through the previous year) and an approximate amount you can expect to receive in retirement. Look carefully at that statement. Make sure that all of the information such as your name is correct. If your name, number, and address are not correct, contact Social Security by phone at 1-800-772-1213 or on the Internet at www.ssa.gov. Then you need to decide if you will be able to live on that amount when you are retired. Keep in mind that your health may not be as good as it is today and that medicine and doctor's appointments may eat up a good portion of that benefit. If your projected Social Security income isn't enough to meet your needs, you will have to supplement it with other retirement savings.

If you work for an employer, find out if they offer retirement programs such as a 401(k) or a 403(b) and how much of your contributions your employer matches. To get the answers, talk to someone in the company's human resources department or in the benefits office. **As soon as possible, you should at least contribute the amount your employer will match.** This should be your first priority once you have a little extra income each month and your emergency savings account has 3-6 months of living expenses in it. This is especially true if your employer matches your contribution—an employer match is free money! Work with a financial advisor to decide which investment option is best for you—usually there are several to choose from. If your company's retirement plan is exclusively invested in company stock, you probably should look for ways to diversify. Just like individuals, companies can and do go bankrupt. If you are self-employed, speak with your accountant to learn what retirement plans are available to you and which plan makes the most sense for you and your employees.

It is also a wise idea to start an *Individual Retirement Account (IRA)*. If you are a taxpayer, you may contribute earnings to an IRA up to a maximum amount each year. Each IRA has different rules, but they all allow your money to grow either tax-deferred or tax free. These are excellent investment tools. Consult a financial advisor, speak with someone at your local bank, or do some research on your own. Tax-deferred or tax-free investments offer every taxpayer big advantages.

Even if your employer offers a company-funded retirement program, you should still set up some type of additional retirement account of your own. In recent years, we have seen several large company and union pension plans go bankrupt and get turned over to the government. The government has limits on the amount it will pay out to reconcile the debt, and those limits may not match your expectations.

Kick your ATM habit.

To pay for all their incidental treats, some people go to their ATM, withdraw $40, $80, or $100, and return the next day because they have spent that money. If this description fits you, keep track of where that money is being spent. Do you really need this much cash every day? You could put yourself on an ATM diet and limit yourself to no more than one or two ATM withdrawals a week. Or, if this is a serious problem for you financially, get rid of the ATM card completely.

Save your small change.

Some people routinely take the change from their pockets or wallets each evening and put it into a drawer, milk bottle, or piggy bank. Then, every so often, they empty it out, convert the change into bills, and get to splurge. To build this nest egg faster, you might stash away the single dollar bills that are left over whenever you break a $10 or $20 bill. We're not talking about funding a vacation, but just paying for a fun time or a nice evening out.

Little things add up.

Ever wonder why you feel you can't get ahead? Stop. Look at the items you buy every day or several times a week. Do you stop on the way to work for a coffee? Do you buy candy or cigarettes on a regular basis? For one week, honestly add up the amounts you are spending then multiply that by the 52 weeks in a year. That's how little things can add up to BIG dollar amounts. For example, saving only $2 per day at a safe bank interest rate of 3 percent would add up to almost $8,400 after 10 years and $19,615 after 20 years. If that money was put into investments that average 8 percent growth a year, the totals would climb to $10,757 after 10 years and more than $33,000 after 20 years.

You do not have to save a lot of money for it to add up—just think every morning whether that cup of coffee or piece of pastry is really worth it. To get an idea of how small savings can add up over the years, check out the Web site "Stop Buying Expensive Coffee and Save Calculator," (www.hughchou.org/calc/coffee.cgi).

The power of compounding.

Albert Einstein called compounding interest the eighth wonder of the world. When compounding works for you, it's wonderful. As you can see from the Coffee Calculator in the previous section, a small amount of money adds up quickly because you earn interest not only on the money you have deposited in the bank but also on the interest you have previously earned. There is a trick though. **You only continue to earn interest on interest as long as you keep your money in the bank or some other investment like a money market fund that pays regular interest.** Every time you draw money from that fund you eliminate much of the benefit of compounding.

Compounding also has a negative effect. When you run up debts, the interest you owe continues to add up. If you don't make your payments on time or stop making payments, late fees and other fees get added on to the money you owe, and interest is charged on the entire amount! If credit card debt was the reason for your bankruptcy, compounding interest certainly played a key role.

"Payday" loans are expensive and dangerous.

You may be tempted to use a payday loan now that you have a bankruptcy on your record. After all, it seems like a convenient way to get much-needed cash even if your credit is bad. Don't do it! To get a payday loan, people usually give the loan company a postdated check for the amount of the loan plus the fees associated with the loan. This looks like a very easy way to get cash to make it to the next paycheck, but what happens if you can't pay with the next paycheck? What happens if you find yourself short again? The payday loan company usually adds a number of other fees. **You could end up paying as much as 400 percent interest using payday loans.**

Payday loans can be the first step back to serious debt problems, and bankruptcy will not be an option again any time soon. Under the law, you will have to wait several years before you can file for bankruptcy again. You are going to have to live with any debts you incur at this time in your life, so you absolutely need to make good choices.

It really is much wiser to make a budget, set up an emergency fund, and stick to your budget. Before you get a payday loan, talk to your nearest credit counselor to see what other alternatives are available.

Balance your checking account every month.

Believe it or not, banks can make mistakes! Money you deposited can be credited to someone else's account, a fee could be charged to your account by mistake, or any of several other mistakes could be made. You will never know if any mistakes were made unless you reconcile your account statement monthly. More importantly, balancing your account is just good money management. You always need to know how much money you have in your checking account. Otherwise, how will you know whether you are within your budget, or falling behind? All it takes is a few unbudgeted expenses or undetected math errors to get you off course. Losing track of your money may have been one reason you wound up in bankruptcy in the first place. If that was a problem, you don't want to make the same mistake again. If you haven't been balancing your account, start now!

Resolve that you will sit down on a certain night after you receive your statement and reconcile the account. The instructions for reconciling are on the back of one of the forms included in your monthly statement. If you have difficulty, you can go into the bank, and someone will help you. If you find a mistake, simply contact your bank and explain to them what you've found. If the mistake resulted in a fee charged to you, ask for it to be repaid. By all means, if it resulted in a check being returned for insufficient funds, ask the bank to write a letter explaining the mistake to the store or person who received the check as well as to the credit reporting agencies.

Organize your bills and save important papers.

Organization is important. This is another vital habit to build as you begin to reshape your financial behavior following bankruptcy. Having a designated time and place to pay bills and store records will give you the assurance that you are in control. Set up your place for paying bills with all of the basics: pen, stamps, work space, and possibly a calendar. If you can't or don't wish to pay your bills as they arrive, a calendar, chart, or list is a must. You need to write on the calendar the due date and the name of the bill you need to pay. (If you use a computer to pay your bills, the software can probably be set up to remind you when a bill is due or to pay it automatically at the same time each month). Be sure to write the check at least a week in advance of the due date to avoid any chance of a late payment that could bring a penalty fee or add a negative entry to your credit report.

You will also need a place to keep important information as well as the proof you've paid the bill. It can be as simple as a box wide enough to comfortably fit manila folders or a file drawer. For the purposes of protecting against identity theft, it would be best if you had a drawer that locked so you can keep your various account numbers secure. You should have a file for each bill you pay. As you pay each bill, record the date you paid it as well as either the check or money order number. This bookkeeping may seem tiresome, but it is an important part of personal money management. In addition to keeping files, you may want to use money management software for maintaining your records. Even if you use a computer, you will need hard copies of many types of documents for complete information and as essential evidence in case of dispute. What should you be saving?

- **Bills.** Bills are a record of what you owe. If the company overcharges you, it will appear on your bill. If you make a payment, it will appear

on your bill. Keep regular bills in a separate file for quick access, and keep occasional bills in one location. Every time you pay a bill, note when you paid it, how much, and the check number or debit card information with which you paid.

- **Insurance policies and bills.** Documents from your insurance companies must be kept. They contain useful numbers in case you need to contact the company as well as a detailed list of your coverage in case the items insured are damaged or lost.

- **Medical insurance and bills.** Retain information about medicine, health insurance coverage, doctor visits, and any ordered medical tests you received.

- **Home improvement or repair receipts.** Keep information about any work you had done on your home or cars. This helps prove that you had the work completed if the work was paid for with insurance proceeds. It can also document improvements that may reduce your taxes when you sell your home.

- **Important documents.** Keep Social Security cards, birth certificates, shot records, medical files, passports, car registrations, dental records, etc. This file should contain any legal documents that identify you or create a contract, such as loan papers.

- **Bank statements.** Keep account statements from your bank. Some people find it convenient to buy a three-hole punch and save these in a notebook.

- **Investment or retirement accounts.** Keep account statements concerning any of your investment accounts. Normally, any investment firm will send you an end-of-year statement that lists all contributions and withdrawals made for the year. Keep monthly or quarterly statements throughout the year, then, when you receive your end-of-year statement, discard the monthly statements for that year. Always keep your end-of-year statements permanently.

Now, with these tips and ideas in mind, let's begin to build a budget that works!

CHAPTER FOUR

My Current Budget: How Did I Get Here?

"Budgets are nothing but a set of oppressive rules that limit my freedom. It's my money and I'll spend it however I want." Sound familiar? That's one of many reasons people avoid budgeting. They see it as a freedom issue. In reality, a budget can actually free you from worries about overspending and debt. Ultimately, your budget may become a source of pride, a clear sign that you are in control and on the right track. Financial experts agree that developing and sticking to a budget are the keys to good money management, yet many people resist the idea of living within a budget. Since money issues forced you to file for bankruptcy, it's time to stop resisting. Before you can begin to create a budget, however, you need two important pieces of information. You need to know what you have been doing with your money and also what financial goals you want to achieve. In this chapter, we'll find out what you've been doing with your money.

Developing Sound Budgeting Skills

In the last chapter, we asked you to answer some questions about your current thinking about money and to discuss your answers with your credit counselor. Now we're going to begin giving you the basic building blocks to take control of your finances. We will start with five basic budgeting skills you should learn to achieve long-term financial wellness. These skills and habits will, in turn, enable you to ultimately achieve your short- and long-term financial goals. Chances are, if you're like most people, at least some of your financial habits can be improved. The next two

chapters will help you do that by improving your budgeting skills, showing you how you are currently spending your money, demonstrating where and how you can make changes to improve your financial situation, and by helping you learn how to live within a budget.

First, let's take a look at the five basic budgeting skills we want you to develop and use. We also ask you to commit to improve these essential skills and to practice them for the rest of your life. Take a few moments to answer the following questions honestly. A "yes" answer is a sound budgeting skill you've already developed. A "no" represents a skill you need to develop to achieve your goals. If you check "no" in any box, resolve here and now to develop that skill. At the end of the next chapter, you will be able to write a specific plan based on these skills which will help you achieve your goals—a plan called a workable budget.

1. **Do I have a written budget that addresses my income and spending?**
   ❑ YES ❑ NO (I **will** create a written budget by _____ and live by it!)

2. **Have I stopped adding to my debts and developed a plan to pay them off?**
   ❑ YES ❑ NO (I **will** stop adding to my debts and create a plan to pay them off!)

3. **Do I save for periodic expenses such as car insurance, car repairs, vacations, and gifts?**
   ❑ YES ❑ NO (I **will** save money for periodic expenses and pay cash!)

4. **Have I set up an emergency savings plan to cover my living expenses for 3-6 months if I become unemployed?**
   ❏ YES   ❏ NO (I **will** save money for emergencies to cover 3-6 months of living expenses!)

5. **Have I created a plan to save for my retirement and major expenses?**
   ❏ YES   ❏ NO (I **will** save for my retirement and major expenses!)

The skills these questions address are the basic building blocks of financial responsibility. Many of us never learned them. Since you are getting a fresh start through bankruptcy, this is an ideal time to begin practicing these skills every day and teaching them to every member of your family. With these skills, you can take control of your personal finances forever. But, if you refuse to learn or use them, you may wind up in financial difficulty again. This is your chance to identify your bad financial habits and change them. Keeping in mind these weaknesses that you have now resolved to turn into strengths, let's find out where you stand financially today. As we begin to examine your current financial situation and build a new budget—one that can actually work—use your credit counselor and the resources listed in the final chapter to guide you along the way. Your credit counselor is your financial coach. Ask questions and follow his or her advice. The objectives of the next two chapters are:

- To help you identify how you are now spending your money;
- To talk with your credit counselor about the factors in your life which have created your current financial problems;

- To identify the areas of your current budget most affected by those factors;
- To learn how to practice sound budgeting skills to address those problems and solve them; and
- To create a new budget plan that will enable you to achieve your financial goals.

Calculating Your Net Worth

Before creating your monthly budget, it's always helpful to have a good sense of where you stand overall with your personal finances. Many times, families have a sense that they have "a little too much" on their credit cards. But this vague sense of a problem is often not enough to trigger real action. On the other hand, when families realize their net worth is *minus* $25,000, they begin to develop a real sense of urgency to change their financial habits.

As a first step, you must list all of your **assets** and all of your **liabilities**. You have already done this as part of the bankruptcy process, but we ask that you do it here again with an eye toward what your financial situation will be once your debts are discharged (or, if you are in Chapter 13 bankruptcy, when your repayment plan ends). This is a new beginning, and we want you to have an accurate starting point. Again, many of the items in this exercise may not apply to you now since much of your debt is about to be removed by your bankruptcy discharge. However, you will revisit this budget periodically from now on, and, as you recover from your bankruptcy, more and more of the items will apply. Develop the habit of doing this inventory regularly—at least once a month at the beginning. Soon, you will begin to have a very accurate idea of where your money is and how you are spending it.

Table 1: Assets

Assets	Value
Cash and Cash Equivalents	
Checking #1	
Checking #2	
Savings #1	
Savings #2	
Certificates of Deposit	
Other	
Investments (non-retirement)	
Mutual Funds (total)	
Stocks (total)	
Bonds (total)	
Savings Bonds (total)	
Retirement Funds	
IRAs (total)	
401(k) (total)	
403(b) (total)	
SEP/SIMPLE (total)	
Company Retirement Plans (vested)	
Real Property	
Home (current market value)	
Land	
Auto #1 (current market value)	
Auto #2 (current market value)	
Motorcycle	
RV/Plane/ATV	
Other	
Household Goods	
Furniture	
Jewelry	
Computers	
Home Entertainment Center	
Tools	
Valuable Collections	
Total Assets	

Table 2: Liabilities

Liabilities	Amount Owed
Long-Term Loans	
Mortgage Amount	
Second Mortgage	
Home Equity Line of Credit	
Student Loan #1	
Student Loan #2	
Consolidation Loan	
Other Bank Loans	
Auto Loan #1	
Auto Loan #2	
Credit Cards	
MasterCard #1	
MasterCard #2	
Discover Card #1	
Discover Card #2	
Visa #1	
Visa #2	
American Express	
Dept. Store #1	
Dept. Store #2	
Dept. Store #3	
Gas (total)	
Taxes Owed	
Income	
Property	
Tax liens	
Misc. Other Debts	
Relatives	
Friends	
Medical Bills	
Checking Account Overdraft Balances	
Payday Loans	
Total Liabilities	
Calculate Your Net Worth	
Total Assets	
Minus Total Liabilities	
Equals Your Net Worth	

Income and Expenses

Now we need to know where you stand with your monthly income and spending. To start this process, you need to figure out exactly how much actual "take-home" or spendable income you receive in one month. Your *gross income* is the total amount of money you earn or receive each month before any *deductions* are taken out of your pay. Deductions include money taken out for federal, state, and local income taxes, Social Security and Medicare taxes. Deductions may also include other mandatory and voluntary payments for such things as spousal maintenance (alimony), child support, retirement plans, health care plans, union dues, and any number of other payments. Your *net income* or "take-home" pay is what's left after all the deductions have been taken out. For the purposes of creating your budget in this book, we are going to define "net income" as your gross income minus withholding for:

1. Federal income taxes
2. State and local income taxes
3. Social Security
4. Medicare

Almost everyone who receives income each month must pay items one, three, and four. Item two is required in some states. For the purposes of building your budget here, list any other deductions from your pay as separate expenses using the following three tables. Now, let's determine how much monthly income you earn. For the moment do NOT fill out the "Necessary Changes" and "Planned Net Income" sections of the table.

How Are You Spending Your Money?

Now that we know how much money is coming in, we need to know where and how you are spending it. For today, you will have to estimate how much you are spending for various items. However, there is no substitute for tracking your actual spending. **Most of us underestimate how much we are actually spending on different items in our budget. The only way to be sure is to track everything you spend for at least two weeks—a month would be better.** You should do this immediately, if you haven't done it already as part of your bankruptcy filing process. Then, once you've tracked your actual

Table 3: Net Monthly Income

Monthly Income Source	Monthly Income		
	Current Monthly Income	Necessary Changes	Planned Net Income
Net Income #1 (income less taxes, Social Security, Medicare)			
Net Income #2 (income less taxes, Social Security, Medicare)			
Net Income #3 (income taxes, Social Security, Medicare)			
Child Support Received			
Spousal Support Received			
Military Retirement			
Other Retirement			
Social Security Received (after taxes)			
Other Income (list source)			
Total Take-Home Income			

spending, revise the budget you will create today so that it's more accurate.

There are several ways to track your daily, weekly, and monthly spending. You might need to combine methods to find what works best for you. To figure out how you spend your money, carry a piece of paper with you and write down where every dollar goes. Total the amount at the end of the day and enter it into the following chart. Do this for at least two weeks—if you can, it would be best to do it for a month. In addition, also keep track of your income on the chart. Every time you receive money, write the amount and the source in the income row. For example, record your paycheck amount on the day you receive it. Record any other income you receive such as gifts, dividends, or any interest payments that come directly to you.

Tracking what you spend is the most important part of this record keeping. Record on your daily list what you purchase and the amount you pay for each purchase. Whenever you pay with cash, write a check, use a credit or debit card, or go online to pay a bill, be sure to record both the amount and the reason on your chart. Remember to record any payments you have automatically taken out of your checking account such as an insurance payment or a health club membership. If you have any fees connected with using online payments, debit cards, or ATM machines, be sure to record them. **Remember: both you and your spouse— and any other members of your family who create income or expenses which affect the family budget—must do this!** At the end of each day, combine each family member's amount on your chart.

At the end of each week, total the amounts you have listed as income and the amounts you have spent. If you are comfortable with computers, you could set up a spreadsheet to track your spending. Your daily tracking chart on page 23.

Three Types of Expenses: Fixed, Variable, and Periodic

Now that you have a better understanding of your overall financial picture, we will focus on your expenses. There are three categories of expenses: *fixed monthly expenses, variable (or discretionary) monthly expenses,* and *periodic (less frequent than monthly) expenses.* Every expense falls into one of these three categories. We will now list all of your expenses in the following tables. A few notes before we begin are in order.

It's important to look at long-term debt very closely because sometimes, simply by selling the property such as a boat or a car that created the debt, you can reduce your monthly expenses and give yourself money to pay off other debts more rapidly. Some of your long-term debt may already have been identified for discharge by your bankruptcy trustee. Other long-term debts may be reaffirmed or non-dischargable, and you will be obligated to pay them off. Include any debts that you plan to reaffirm or which you think may be non-dischargable in the following tables depending on the type of debt.

The next important category you need to look at in detail is credit card debt. This is very often a leading cause of personal bankruptcies, so we want to examine it very closely in order to better appreciate its impact on your overall budget. Again, while the pending discharge of your debts may eliminate credit card debt right now, you may begin using credit cards again in the future. It is critical that you learn how to identify and manage credit cards because they are very easy to abuse.

Because you control how much you spend using credit cards and how much to pay each month, we will list credit card debts under "Variable Monthly Expenses." For your "Current Monthly Payment" on each credit card, list the minimum payment

Table 4: Daily Expense Tracking Sheet

	Sunday	Monday	Tuesday	Wednesday	Thursday	Friday	Saturday
Income: Date/ Amount/ Source Full Month							
Expenses Item/ Amount Week 1							
Week 2							
Week 3							
Week 4							
Week 5							

amount required. If you don't know it, list the average amount you paid over the past three months. Obviously, if all of your credit card debt is about to be discharged through your bankruptcy, you will have no entries to make for now.

Category 1: Monthly Fixed Expenses

These are regular, known expenses that must be paid each month. The amounts may vary somewhat, but generally they are within a small range. They represent payments that must be made in order for you to receive vital services or to pay off long-term debt. If you have filed for a *Chapter 7 bankruptcy* and have reaffirmed any debts, or if you have filed Chapter 13 and are now on a debt repayment plan, you should include those payments in Table 5 on page 25.

Notice we include here payments to a retirement fund and payments to an emergency savings account. Depending on your income, you may not have the money for these items right now. However, these payments are so vital to your long-term financial health that you should strive to include them in your budget. Once you have the money for these types of funds, you should arrange to have it taken out of your pay **before you receive it** and have it deposited automatically into accounts that are set aside only for these specific purposes. This is a way to put into action the rule to "Pay Yourself First" before you are tempted to spend it in some less important way.

Use the daily lists of your expenditures to calculate the monthly totals for each of the categories listed below.

Category 2: Monthly Savings for Periodic Expenses

These are also expenses that are vital to sustain your daily living, but that don't occur every month. They can seriously affect your monthly budget if you haven't saved for them in advance. Think about those expenses, such as insurance or taxes that you pay quarterly, semi-annually, or annually. The best way to deal with them is to set aside a specific amount of money each month so that the bill doesn't catch you without enough money to pay it. Ideally, this money should be set aside in an account separate from your regular checking account so you are less likely to spend it. In Table 6 on page 26 we will calculate a monthly amount you need to save for each periodic expense.

Category 3: Monthly Variable Expenses

Finally, it's time to list those expenses over which you have the most control and for which you can more easily increase or decrease spending. Many people refer to these as Variable Expenses. Use your income/expense record, checkbook register, or receipts to record the amounts you actually spend in the various categories. Some of these expenses occur daily. Here again, your daily lists of how much you actually spent can help you fill in the amounts. Simply add each type of expense for the entire month and put the total on Table 7 on page 27.

Assessing Your Current Monthly Situation

You have gathered a great deal of information about your finances. It's time to put everything together and get the whole picture. Do that by transferring the totals from the bottom lines of the table on page 29 to the **"Where You Stand"** table below. Now you can see at a glance whether you have extra income or are going further into debt each month. Ideally, since you are about to have your debts discharged, you will have a surplus. But if your expenses exceed your income even after the debt discharge, you are going to have to make some adjustments immediately. **If you are in that circumstance, you should speak to your credit counselor immediately to identify changes necessary for your financial health.** You do not want to run up new debts so soon after bankruptcy. Another bankruptcy filing may not be an option because of restrictions on repeated discharges. And, even if you could file for bankruptcy again, it is unlikely that you want to repeat the experience.

Table 5: Monthly Fixed Expenses

Monthly Fixed Expenses	Current Monthly Spending	Necessary Changes	Planned Budget
Mortgage #1			
Mortgage #2			
Auto Loan/Lease # 1			
Auto Loan/Lease # 2			
RV Loan			
Home Equity Loan			
Debt Consolidation/Other Loan(s)			
Student Loan(s)			
Rent			
Condo or Homeowner Association Fees			
Electricity			
Oil or Gas Heat			
Water			
Garbage Collection			
Sewer			
Phone (land line)			
Cell Phones, Pagers, PDA			
Cable/Satellite TV/TiVo Boxes			
Internet Access			
Car Insurance			
Health Insurance (if it isn't deducted from your paycheck)			
Long-Term Care Insurance			
Child Support			
Alimony			
Medical/Dental Payments			
Retirement Savings			
Emergency Fund Savings			
Other:			
Total Monthly Fixed Expenses			

Table 6: Monthly Savings for Periodic Expenses

Monthly Savings for Periodic Expenses (You save a certain amount each month)	Total Annual Amount	Monthly Amount Saved (annual/12)	Necessary Changes	Planned Budget
Property Taxes (if not in your mortgage payment)				
School Taxes (if not in your mortgage payment)				
State and Local Taxes (if not deducted from your paycheck)				
Quarterly Income Taxes				
Insurance (if not monthly)				
Car Registration/License Tag Renewal				
Car Maintenance				
Home Repair				
Water (if not monthly)				
Sewer (if not monthly)				
Garbage (if not monthly)				
Medical (not regular)				
Dental (not regular)				
Veterinarian				
Gifts				
Vacation/Travel				
Tuition and School Costs				
Memberships				
Charitable Donations (one time)				
Other:				
Other:				
Other:				
Other:				
Total Monthly Periodic Expenses				

Table 7: Monthly Variable Expenses

Total Monthly Variable Expenses (Spending you can change)	Current Spending	Necessary Changes	Planned Budget
Card #1			
Card #2			
Card #3			
Card #4			
Card #5			
Store Card(s) (total)			
Gas Card(s) (total)			
Other Credit Lines Not Included in Table #5			
Groceries			
Eating Out (include restaurants, fast food, lunches, etc)			
School Lunches			
Gasoline, Tolls, Parking			
Public Transportation — Bus, Train, Subway			
Health Club Membership			
Daily Coffee/Snacks			
Laundry/Dry Cleaning			
Household Items (not grocery)			
Pet Care and Supplies			
Baby Items			
Children's Allowances			
Hair Cuts/Grooming/Manicures, etc.			
Cosmetics			
Clothes			
Entertainment:			
Movie			
Movie/Game Rental			
Cable On-Demand Movies			
Sports Event: Games, Races			
Concerts			
Play/Dinner Theater			
Symphony			
Day Trips to Amusement Parks			
Other			
CDs			
Club Dues			
Babysitter/Day Care			

(continued next page)

Table 7: Monthly Variable Expenses (continued)

Total Monthly Variable Expenses (Spending you can change)	Current Spending	Necessary Changes	Planned Budget
Lessons: Music/Sports/Tutoring			
Field Trips			
ATM Withdrawals (if you have not already listed elsewhere what you spent the money on)			
ATM Fees			
Computer/Online Expenses			
Donations/Tithe			
Lawn Service			
Occupational Licenses/Fees			
Emergency Savings			
Retirement Savings			
Tobacco/Alcohol			
Magazine Subscriptions			
Misc. Spending Money			
Postage			
Other:			
Other:			
Total Monthly Variable Expenses			

Table 8: Where You Stand

Summing It All Up			
	Current ($)	Necessary Changes ($)	Planned ($)
1. Total Monthly Take-Home Income (from Table 3)			
2. Total Monthly Fixed Expenses (from Table 5)			
3. Subtract Line 2 from Line 1			
4. Total Monthly Savings for Periodic Expenses (from Table 6)			
5. Subtract Line 4 from Line 3			
6. Total Monthly Variable Expenses (from Table 7)			
7. Subtract Line 6 from Line 5			
The amount on line 7 is your **Surplus** if it is **positive** OR your **Shortage** if it is **negative**.			

CHAPTER FIVE:

My New Budget: Developing a Plan That Works

Now that you have calculated your current income and expenses, you're ready to build a new, smarter budget that puts you in charge of your finances and will help you achieve your personal financial goals. This chapter helps you through that process by asking you to set goals and look for ways to increase income and cut expenses. It also provides you with financial tips and important "rules to live by."

What Are Your Goals?

Before you begin to build a budget that works, spend some time figuring out what your vision of financial security is and how you intend to achieve it. In other words, set some goals for yourself. People who have set, written goals are more successful than those who do not have set goals. This is true regardless of your education and background. That's because when you establish well thought-out goals—goals that truly mean a great deal to you and your family—you'll be better able to overcome obstacles along the way.

Some experts divide goals into short-, medium-, and long-term. A short-term goal can be reached within six months to one year. It could be something like: *I will save enough money to use cash or a check to pay for a vacation to the beach in seven months.* A medium-term goal is something to aim for in one-to-five years. A long-term goal, like saving for a child's education or planning to retire at age 60, is five or more years in the future.

Your goals should be very specific and should help you visualize success. If you want to live in a house that's paid for, state where that house is, what it looks like, and how much it costs in today's dollars. Don't let the fact that you've declared bankruptcy discourage you. You're on a new path now, and having a clear picture of where you want to go is the first step.

The following categories will help you think of goals that are important to you. You need not have a goal listed under each category.

Developing good financial habits: Pick one or two ways you can improve your financial well-being.

Savings: What are your short- and long-term savings goals?

Housing: Where do you want to live?

Transportation: What kinds of transportation would you like to someday have?

Vacation: How much do you want to travel?

Retirement: When do you want to retire and how much money will you need?

Once you have established your goals, you can then build a budget that is designed to achieve each goal It's also a good idea to revisit your goals each year. As you examine each goal, decide whether:

1. You have achieved that goal.
2. You are making progress toward the goal, even though you haven't yet achieved it.
3. You have not made any progress toward the goal.
4. Your ideas have changed and you want to change your goal or add new goals.
5. Your goals are realistic.

If you find you haven't made any progress toward a goal, you need to ask yourself why. Is the goal still important to you? If not, get rid of it. Does the goal need some fine tuning? If so, do it. Maybe the plan to reach the goal needs adjustment. Perhaps you've set a time frame that is too short for your goal.

Since you're just now emerging from bankruptcy, you might want to start with several small, short-term goals that make sense for your current financial situation and can be achieved in fairly short order. Short-term success can help reinforce your commitment to stick with your budget plan. It also may give you the confidence to set more ambitious, but still realistic, long-term goals.

What Factors Are Causing the Biggest Problems?

Now that you've established where your money is going, you should go back to Chapter 4 and review each item in your current budget. Where are you spending the most money? Having gone through the bankruptcy process, circle those areas that caused the greatest problems and talk with your counselor about how to manage those areas better in the future. Ask yourself the following questions:

1. Into what large categories does most of my spending fall? (Groceries, eating at restaurants, utilities—electricity, gas, water, land phone, cell phone, cable—car expenses and other transportation, etc.?)

2. Everyone has situations arise that they don't anticipate. Which of my items represent financial emergencies (e.g. car repairs, emergency dental or medical expenses, etc.) for which I was not reimbursed? How much did I spend?
3. An often repeated statement is that nothing is certain but death and taxes. For most of us there are also gift-giving occasions—birthdays, Mother's and Father's Days, holidays, graduations—you name it, and it frequently requires you to bring a gift. Did I purchase too many gifts or were they too expensive? For whom did I buy, and how much did I spend?
4. What quarterly, semi-annual, or annual expenses such as income taxes (self-employed), personal property taxes, property insurance, car insurance, renters' or homeowners' insurance did I have? Which ones caught me by surprise? What and how much were they? When did they occur?
5. Now think about where you spent your money and how that correlates with the goals you just set for yourself. What did I do in the past month to help me attain those goals? For example, now that I have a fresh start, would I rather stay out of debt or take an expensive vacation?
6. Did I have expenses that, while enjoyable, might be considered luxuries that I could have done without or that could have been replaced with a less costly alternative?
7. Which of the items in my spending record actually helped to increase my wealth? Try highlighting them with a color highlighter or putting a star next to them in another color.

To get the most from this exercise you must discuss the specific factors that caused your financial problems with your certified credit counselor. Some factors, like a period of unemployment, may have been beyond your control, but you also may have made bad choices. Whatever the specific circumstances of your bankruptcy, taking control of your future financial life requires an honest and thorough review of your pre-bankruptcy budget and a recognition of problem areas that need to be addressed.

Ideas for Increasing Income or Reducing Expenses

By now, you and your credit counselor have already identified some ways to increase income and reduce expenses. The list that follows is intended to provide additional ideas. Use it to help you to think of ways that will help you the most, but remember that some of the things you think will help increase your income might have an additional cost attached to them. For example, if you choose to take a second job, will you also face higher child care costs? It's best to examine choices from all angles to be sure they will work for you.

Increase income
(check those you can try)

- ❑ Get a second job in the evenings or on weekends
- ❑ Look for a better-paying job
- ❑ Market any skills you have as a consultant, or give lessons in an area you know (in addition to your full-time job)
- ❑ See if another family member can get a part-time job
- ❑ For a short time, contribute less to your 401(k) or other retirement plan
- ❑ Get a roommate if you have extra space
- ❑ Rent out a room, garage, or barn
- ❑ Sell an asset
- ❑ Sell an unneeded vehicle, collectable, or some other possession
- ❑ Obtain entitlements for which you are qualified (Medicaid, SSI, WIC, utility assistance, education, and food stamps)
- ❑ Use assistance for medical bills (apply at hospitals and offices for assistance)
- ❑ Seek legal ways to obtain court-ordered child support
- ❑ Change your withholding allowance★

★Here are some ideas about changing the amount of taxes being withheld from your pay to "increase" your income. First, reducing your withholding amount (by increasing your exemptions on your W-4 form) does not increase your income; it reduces the amount of taxes you pay each month. This has the effect of increasing your monthly take-home amount. If you reduce your withholding too much—that is, have too few taxes taken out each month—you may be faced with a major tax bill next April. On the other hand, many people use their withholding amount as forced savings and have more taxes withheld than is necessary. We all like to receive a nice, big refund check in April. However, you should understand that your refund check is essentially an interest-free loan you are making to the government. Rather than loan money unnecessarily to the government, why not adjust your withholding amount so that you receive a modest refund—say a few hundred dollars—and use the extra monthly take-home amount created by the lower tax withholdings to increase the monthly amount you are saving or investing. You should meet with a financial advisor or tax specialist to determine the proper amount of taxes to withhold based on your situation.

One more note on taxes. Many tax preparers now offer to pay customers their tax refunds immediately and allow the customer to have a refund check deposited directly into the tax preparer's account when it arrives. This is a loan, and the tax preparers charge a fee for this service which can be very expensive! Better to be patient and save yourself some money.

Reduce expenses
(check those you can try)

First look at where you now spend "out of pocket" cash or debit card money. When you filed for bankruptcy and first examined your budget, were you surprised at how much you were actually spending? Now, as part of your new, financially sound lifestyle, can you:

- ❑ Make coffee at home and take it with you?
- ❑ Carry your lunch instead of eating out at work?
- ❑ Wash your own car?
- ❑ Wax your own car?
- ❑ Skip a manicure or two?

- ❏ Do your own yard work?
- ❏ Clip coupons and use them at the grocery store?
- ❏ Rent a movie instead of going to a theater?
- ❏ End either your cell phone service or your land line?
- ❏ Reduce phone plans to the bare essentials?
- ❏ Eliminate cell phone overtime charges?
- ❏ Use a low-cost calling card for long distance telephone calls?
- ❏ Comparison shop for auto insurance, long distance, and Internet service?
- ❏ Cancel premium movie channels?
- ❏ Cancel memberships in CD or DVD clubs?
- ❏ Cancel cable, TiVo, or satellite television completely?
- ❏ Refinance your car at a lower interest rate?
- ❏ Sell a car because you can car pool or use mass transit?
- ❏ Reduce child care expenses?
- ❏ Reduce insurance expenses by increasing deductibles or qualifying for discounts (low mileage, vehicle safety, good student, good driver, accident free, multi-vehicle)?
- ❏ Use a grocery list to help eliminate impulse purchases?
- ❏ Use bonus cards, coupons, and sales flyers?
- ❏ Shop more often or exclusively at discount stores?
- ❏ Limit yourself to a specific amount of spending money each week?
- ❏ Limit yourself to one ATM withdrawal per week?
- ❏ Cancel Private Mortgage Insurance (PMI) because you owe less than 80 percent of the appraised value of your home?
- ❏ Carefully track your spending?
- ❏ Control impulse spending?
- ❏ Reduce the number of packs of cigarettes you buy, if you smoke? Or give up smoking entirely?
- ❏ Have each family member write down how he/she can reduce spending and costs?
- ❏ Stop playing the lottery?

Changing Your Financial Behavior: Creating a New Budget Based on Sound Financial Skills

Remember the five questions at the beginning of Chapter Four? They represent the basic budgeting skills you must develop to achieve your goals. Before you go back and make changes to your existing budget to address the problem areas you and your counselor have identified, review the tips below. These will help you and your counselor personalize these core skills to your own circumstances. Then, using these tips, revise your current monthly budget by making entries in the "Necessary Changes" column to create a new and better budget that will help you meet your goals.

Skill #1: I will create a written budget by _____ and live by it!

Here are useful tips to help you set priorities before you revise your plan:

- **Pay yourself first.** If your income exceeds your expenses, you should be saving or investing money every month. As noted previously, put this money in the proper accounts immediately after you receive your monthly income (have it deducted automatically if possible). If you're self-employed, develop the habit of depositing this amount at the start of every month.
- **Always pay housing-related expenses right after you've paid yourself.** Mortgage payments, rent, real estate taxes, homeowners or renters insurance, mobile home lot payments, condo fees, and similar living expenses are at the top of the list. You must have a place to live.
- **Next, pay family necessities and utility services.** You and your family need to eat, and utilities such as water, gas, oil, and electricity *must* be paid on time. Try to conserve wherever possible.

- **Pay car loans and leases as long as you keep your car.** Just as your house is *collateral* for your mortgage, your car is collateral for your car loan. Paying your car loan is a high priority. In most parts of the country, a car is a necessity. Even if you plan to sell your car, you have a legal obligation to make the payments until you sell it. Otherwise, your car might be repossessed, and you may further damage your credit.

- **Always pay child support payments.** These are court-ordered payments that must be made. Failure to pay child support is a crime that can put you in jail.

- **Income tax debts must be paid.** The government has collection rights that other creditors do not have. It is also important to file your tax return, even if you cannot pay. Non-filing is usually worse than non-payment. In addition, many tax debts are not discharged by bankruptcy.

- **Student loan payments are important.** These debts are usually not discharged by bankruptcy. They also have special collection options like *garnishment* of your income tax refund if they haven't been paid. There are many deferral and repayment options available when student loans are in default. Be sure to check these out thoroughly.

- **Loans without collateral may be adjusted by working with creditors.** Not paying an *unsecured debt* such as a credit card bill will damage your credit report and your credit score. However, you may be able to work with the holders of your unsecured credit to reduce your payments or interest. If you work with your creditors, the consequences of not paying these debts, while serious, are not normally as severe as a failure to pay a *secured debt*.

- **Refinancing a loan to get new cash does not usually solve the problem.** Ask yourself, "Will refinancing solve my problem, or just take care of it for the time being?" **You cannot borrow your way out of debt.**

If you borrow frequently to make ends meet and make no other adjustments to your lifestyle and habits, you are only getting deeper into trouble and delaying the inevitable.

Skill #2: I will stop adding to my debts and develop a plan to pay them off!

- **Shopping is not a way to improve your self-image.** If you find yourself spending money to make yourself feel better or to get a short-term emotional boost, financial trouble is a very real possibility. Try asking yourself, "Will buying this item really make my life better? Will my life suffer without it?" If you charge the item and only make minimum monthly payments, the debt may last longer than the item you just bought. If your spending problem is serious, you may need to seek professional help.

- **You can't eliminate all fun.** As you go through and make cuts in your budget, do not completely eliminate entertainment or personal spending money. A budget that does is doomed to failure. Everyone should have some money to spend for pleasure.

- **Use the "Power Payment" method to eliminate debt in a structured way.** Because bankruptcy may have eliminated most if not all of your debts, you may not need to use this tool now. However, if you are making payments to any reaffirmed accounts, you can use the power payment method to make larger repayments than required and eliminate your debt sooner. This method of eliminating debt goes by several different names and has been around for a very long time. There are two rules that must be followed:

Rule # 1 **You cannot borrow more money for any reason.**

Rule # 2 **You must find a way to set up an "emergency cash fund."**

Power Payment Schedule

Credit Card (List beginning with the lowest balance)	Balance due	Amount I Will Pay	Date Paid Off
1.			
2.			
3.			
4.			
5.			
6.			
7.			
8.			
9.			
10.			
Car Loan			
Car Loan			
Car Loan			
Mortgage			
Mortgage			
Other			

Here is how the "Power Payment" method works:

1. The goal is to create extra monthly income as fast as possible by reducing your total debt. If you would like to use a chart solely for your "Power Payment" plan, one is provided for you on the last page of this chapter. **Pay the minimum amounts on every debt you owe, but pay the maximum amount your are able on the debt with the lowest balance.** If you are in the habit of not paying close attention to the minimum amount due, start checking it. Some banks are increasing these minimum payments in response to directives from government regulators. **However, you should pay extra only if you can SAVE in your emergency fund at the same time.** Keep doing this until the first debt is paid in full.

2. After the first debt is paid, add the money you were paying on the first debt to the regular payment you have been making on the next lowest debt. **Any time you have a choice between two roughly equal debts, pay the one with the higher interest rate first.** Continue in this manner until the second debt is paid, then the third, and so forth. The rolling of payments from debts that are paid off into other debts that have "balances" is the "Power Payment."

3. For real emergencies, use the Emergency Savings Fund recommended earlier in this book. When that happens, stop sending your "Power Payments" and go back to sending the minimum payments to your creditors. Divert the extra money from your "Power Payments" into replenishing your emergency fund. As soon as the emergency fund has been replenished, go back to making "Power Payments."

4. Keep adding the amount of the payment from debts that are paid off into the remaining debt

repayments. Just keep going from one balance to another. Getting rid of your debts won't happen overnight, but you didn't accumulate them overnight. **Some people have found that "Power Payments" can eliminate debt in less than one-third of the time it would take paying minimum payments.** Once these debts are taken care of, you can use "Power Payments" on car and mortgage loans as well. Paying extra on big loans will pay them off years early and can save you thousands of dollars in interest charges.

5. **Make sure your payments arrive before the due date to avoid penalties. This means that any bill with a due date during a weekend should be paid by Friday, the week prior, if mailed.** Late payments result in late charges and can further hurt your credit rating.

Skill #3: I will save for periodic (less frequent than monthly) expenses and pay cash!

We addressed this in the last chapter. Remember, people who haven't planned for this type of expense often use credit to pay periodic expenses, typically putting their finances under even greater stress.

Skill #4: I will set up an emergency savings plan to cover my living expenses for three-to-six months to protect myself from a surprise like losing my job.

Think of your savings account as your shock absorber for life. We can't predict what life throws at us financially, but we can plan ahead to limit the financial impact of the unexpected.

Skill #5: I will save for my retirement and major expenses.

Remember, the bigger the goal, the earlier in life you must begin saving to achieve that goal. Use the power of compound interest to achieve your dreams. A rule of thumb in the financial planning industry is: "If you want to retire comfortably, invest 10 percent every month; if you want to retire early, invest 15 percent every month; if you want to retire rich, invest 20 percent every month!"

Rework your budget

Now that you've reviewed the above tips, it's time to go back and rework your budget. Clearly, you have already done this as part of the bankruptcy process; however, it is important to review your post-bankruptcy budget in light of what you have learned in this course. Note any changes you decide to make in the "Necessary Changes" column and note how that affects your new budget. For example if you decided to carpool instead of driving to work, your chart might look like the one below:

Review each budget item with an eye toward reducing your monthly expenses wherever possible. Even though you've done this as part of your bankruptcy, do it again to see if you can't find more surplus dollars available each month to save or invest. Again, make sure your budget includes emergency savings, savings for goals, savings for periodic payments and a reasonable level of entertainment. Remember to keep your goals in mind, and do everything you can to avoid any new borrowing until you are successfully living within your budget and beginning to build wealth.

Monthly Variable Expenses Spending You Can Change	Current Spending	Necessary Changes	Planned Budget
Auto Gas	$120	Reduce $95	$25

CHAPTER SIX

Understanding and Using Credit

Introduction

While you may have decided as a result of your bankruptcy never to use credit again, it is very likely that at some point in your future, credit will again become a reasonable option for you. For this reason, it's important to understand the basics of using credit wisely. Used properly, credit and credit cards offer genuine convenience for everyone in our society. Used without enough care, they can create a financial nightmare. Additionally, your children will almost certainly have access to easy credit while they are still teenagers. You will want to help them learn to use credit wisely. Understanding and using credit prudently is an essential money management skill.

There are some significant advantages to using credit. Major acquisitions such as a car or a house would not be possible for most people without borrowing. Other expensive assets such as furniture or computers may also require the use of credit. Credit cards offer convenience, are safer than carrying large amounts of cash, and can be used almost anywhere in the world. They also make it easier to conduct transactions online, which may enable you to acquire goods at lower prices or more conveniently than going to a physical store.

But unwise or excessive use of credit can lead to substantial financial problems. Using a credit card often does not "feel" like really spending money, which makes it easy to forget exactly how much you have charged. It can also encourage a shopping spree that can leave a long-term financial hangover. The ease of using a credit card can lead to impulse spending and deprive you of money that should be used to build wealth through savings and investment. Unless you can pay off credit card bills in full at the end of each month, credit cards make your purchases more expensive in the long run because of interest charges and other fees.

Credit trouble is a serious problem in the United States, even among people who do not end up in bankruptcy:

- In 2003, total average household credit card debt in the U.S. was $9,205; in the 1990's, it was $2,966;[1]
- In the fourth quarter of 2003, credit card delinquencies hit an all-time high;[2]
- In 2003, total national debt grew by more than 8 percent; 42 percent of that was household debt;[3]
- Estimated 2003 interest payments paid by consumers: $80 Billion;[4] and
- Total credit card fees paid by consumers in 2003: $31 Billion.[5]

[1]CardWeb.com, Feb. 2004
[2]CBS Marketwatch.com, April 2004
[3]U.S. Federal Reserve Web site
[4]CBS Marketwatch.com, April 2004
[5]CBS Marketwatch.com, April 2004

Types and Sources of Credit and Loans

There are three basic types of credit:

- **Cash loans.** This is a loan, usually from a bank or a credit union, with a fixed payback period. It may or may not be paid back with fixed payments. The most significant of these are mortgage or car loans that enable people to buy expensive assets and pay for them over time. A *home equity loan* provides another way to obtain a fixed amount of cash based upon the amount of *equity* (the difference between the home's market value and what you still owe on the mortgage) you have in your home. This type of loan usually has a fixed rate of interest and is paid off with regular monthly payments over a set period of time like your regular mortgage loan. Or, you may get cash by arranging for a financial institution to grant you a *home equity line of credit.* With a line of credit, the lender may give you a checkbook or an electronic card that enables you to use your home equity to pay for items on the spot. It works very much like a credit card. Each time you write a check or use the card you are really borrowing money. Home equity lines of credit usually have a floating or variable interest rate tied to certain publicly-known interest rates set by the government or financial markets. These rates can go up or down, but when they go up they can greatly increase the cost of credit. It's important to remember that your house is collateral that secures the loan. If you don't make your payments on time, the lender can take your house to satisfy the debt. Home equity loans should be used with extreme care.

- **Retail credit cards (store cards).** These are credit cards that allow you to purchase an item on credit from the retailer that issued the card, take the item home immediately, and then begin paying for the item later. Unlike bank credit cards (MasterCard, Visa, Discover, American Express, etc.), the store cards can normally only be used at specific retail stores which issued that card. Many times, these types of purchases come with a "no interest, no payments" promise for a certain number of months (terms vary). **These can be good deals when used properly, but can be very harmful if you're not careful.** For one thing, these installment loans may carry very high interest rates, often as high as 20 percent. Second, it is very easy to get used to no payments and forget to include them in your future budget. When the first payment comes due many months later, you may not be prepared and will have to scramble for the money. The best way to approach these types of arrangements is to begin paying the principal right away and try to pay the full amount before the interest charge is applied. Be aware, however, that these arrangements sometimes only defer the interest. Even though you don't have to pay the interest for 12 months, the retailer keeps track of how much interest you would be charged each month. If you still owe the debt at the end of 12 months, all of the past deferred interest is then added to your account. This can be thousands of dollars in interest depending upon the size of your purchase, so it is very important to truly understand the exact terms of the transaction.

- **Bank credit cards.** These are major, national credit cards (MasterCard, Visa, Discover, American Express, etc.) that can be used anywhere. Bank cards normally have a lower interest rate than store cards, but they can still be very expensive. You may be offered a very low introductory rate such as zero percent interest for six months but get hit with a 19 percent interest rate six months later. Bank cards may also require an annual fee. Finally, be careful of hidden costs. Credit card issuers may raise your interest rate immediately for a late payment. They also may have transfer fees for transferred balances. Finally, read the small print of your credit card agreement. A "*universal default*" clause allows the credit card issuer to raise your interest rate if you default on any account whether or not the account is with that credit card issuer. Such clauses are becoming increasingly common.

The Cost of Credit: Watch Out for Fees

Creditors don't loan you money for free. They charge you interest on your loan and compute it on an annual basis. This is referred to as the *APR* or annual percentage rate. This rate must be disclosed to you before you sign for a loan of any kind. You can be charged **simple interest** or **compound interest**. Simple interest is charged each month only on the **principal**, the amount you actually borrowed. Compound interest is charged on the amount you borrowed **plus** any interest previously added to your loan that you have not paid. This increases the amount you owe much faster than simple interest. Credit card companies charge compound interest.

To illustrate this point, suppose you made a payment of $100 each month to pay off a $5,000 loan at 9 percent simple interest. It would take you just over six years to pay off the loan, and you would pay $1,292.31 in interest charges. On the other hand, if you made the minimum payment of $100 on a $5,000 balance with compound interest, it would take you 246 months—that's 20.5 years—to pay off your loan, and you would pay a total of $2,829.01 in interest. That's $2,829.01 of wasted money that you could have saved, invested, or used for a down-payment on a wealth-building asset like a home.

Additionally, most lenders will charge you fees as part of the loan contract, and you should account for these in determining the true cost of the loan. Payment plans and credit card companies can charge late fees, transfer fees, and annual membership fees. They can dramatically increase the cost of credit to you. And again, creditors can also raise your interest rate significantly if you don't pay on time.

Bank loans may also have fees. Many banks charge *origination fees* for loans. These fees and any number of other bank fees are supposed to cover administrative costs of the loan, but they are usually negotiable. They can be very high, so be careful and make sure the lender fully discloses what those fees are. Don't be afraid to simply say, "I'm not going to pay that fee." The worst that can happen is that you don't get the loan. Shopping for loans and credit cards is wise. Always read the small print, and, if something seems too expensive, ask a credit counselor for advice.

Strategies for Using Credit

As discussed previously, one of the greatest challenges we face using credit cards is that using them does not "feel" like spending money. Through advertising and the media, society tells us that if we want it, we can have it. Yet if we are going to learn to live within a budget, we must completely re-think our use of credit. Here are some tips to help you change the way you think about and use credit:

Use debit cards rather than credit cards.

A debit card gives you the flexibility of a credit card but feels like you're spending cash. It comes right out of your checking account immediately. Here are some suggestions when using debit cards:

- **One person/one account.** If two people are debiting the same account, neither one knows how much money is in the account. If it's a joint account, you will need a system for keeping a single record of transactions. Mistakes or omissions are more likely in that situation.
- **Keep your receipts.** Your receipts enable you to keep track of your transactions. You must keep them to be able to balance the account.
- **Keep track of the paper checks you write on a debit account.** The key to using a debit card wisely is to keep close tabs on your transactions. That can require a bit of effort because you are probably writing some paper checks as well as making electronic transactions. You need to keep track of both, preferably in a single register.
- **Have limited overdraft protection on a debit card account if you don't plan to write any checks on the account.** Many banks have overdraft protection by which an overdraft simply turns your

debit card into a credit card. While it seems convenient, it's really a bad idea when you are trying to stick to a budget. Try to avoid these by setting your card up so that, when the money is gone from the account, the card stops working. In other words, if the money is not in the account, you can't spend it. This only works well if you don't write checks on the account. If you do, overdraft protection is a must.

Limit the number of credit cards you own and carry.

Use just one card if you can. If you need one for business, work with two—one for personal use and one for business use. Even three cards may be fine, especially if each one has a specific purpose. But the fewer you have, the easier it is to remember your balance and keep track of total purchases. The more cards you have, the more likely the cumulative balance will get too large for safety.

Pay off your monthly credit card balance in full.

If you can't pay the balance in full, you should at least resolve to pay more than the minimum while you work off the debt. Paying twice the minimum is a good initial goal to start with. By increasing your payments you will work off the balance faster and reduce the total amount of money that you will pay out over the long term. What's more, credit card companies can raise their minimum payment requirements. If you are just managing the minimum payment now, you could be in deep trouble if the minimum goes up. So, it's a good idea to get used to paying more.

Most important of all is to focus on long term goals and keep your credit card expenditures low and within your budget. If your goal is to save or invest 10 percent of your income each month, and you spend too much on credit cards, you will use part of that 10 percent to pay your credit card bill.

Yes, you will avoid paying interest if you pay the card off entirely. That's a great first step. However, if you have not actually budgeted the amount you spend on credit cards, you are robbing your future to indulge yourself now.

Read Your Monthly Credit Card Statements.

If you are using a credit card, you should read your statements when they arrive every month. It's a good habit to keep all charge receipts. Put them into a folder when you get home from shopping. When your statement arrives, check the statement against the receipts. This way you can make sure that all of the charges are yours. You also can account for the charges by categories in your budget rather than by having one large expense called "credit card."

If there are charges that you are certain neither you nor anyone else in your family have made, you should dispute the transaction as described on the back of the statement. The law requires that disputes be submitted in writing to the financial institution that issued the card. You can usually request to see a copy of the transaction slip as a starting point. You should not be charged interest or late fees for that item while the situation is being resolved.

Your monthly statement also provides information such as your interest rate and fees that may have been assessed on your account. Check these out. You may be paying a higher rate of interest than you thought you were.

If you purchased something at a promotional interest rate, make sure you check the bottom of the statement to find out what interest is being charged on what portion of your charges. Make sure the card issuer is applying the promotional rate correctly. If you have questions, call the card issuer at the number provided on the statement.

Warning Signs of Credit Trouble

You are about to have your debts discharged. The last thing you want to do now is slide back into financial trouble by using credit foolishly. To help you stay on track once you are again using credit (ideally you will wait until you can get credit with reasonable interest rates and on reasonable terms), you will need to spot warning signs of improper credit use. If poor use of credit was a contributing factor to your bankruptcy, be sure you don't make the same bad decisions again. Here are some signs that you may be falling into credit trouble:

- Spending more than 20 percent of your take-home income on credit card bills.
- Borrowing money to pay off other debts.
- Paying your bills on time, but running out of cash between paychecks.
- Using your credit card to pay for necessities because you do not have the cash.
- Paying only the minimum payment on your credit cards; if you can't double the minimum payment, you have a problem.
- Refinancing a loan to get cash or because you need to reduce your payment. Refinancing to reduce a monthly payment because interest rates have declined can be a smart financial move. But if you are refinancing for extra cash because you are over-extended or because you can no longer make the current monthly payment, you are probably in trouble.
- Needing a co-signer may be a warning sign. If the lender requires a co-signer to make a loan creditworthy, you could be over-extended. However, if you need a co-signer because you lack a credit history or because of your bankruptcy, this is not necessarily a problem. Bottom line: make sure you understand why the lender wants a co-signer.

- Financing your vehicle for six or more years, which means you may be paying off the loan longer than you drive the car. This probably means you are buying a more expensive car than you should. **Although a longer loan period reduces your *monthly* payment, it increases the amount you pay over the full term of the loan.** If you can afford a larger monthly payment, it will save you money in the long run.
- Consolidating your loans (including credit card debts), but not closing at least some of the accounts in which those loans originated. By keeping all of those accounts open you may be tempted to compound your problem by using them again and creating new debt.
- Counting on the next "big deal" to see you through your financial trouble; consider the big deal as icing on the cake rather than something to bail you out.
- Carrying more than three credit cards; there is no reason to have more than two or three credit cards.
- Waiting until near the end of your credit card's grace period to pay, or requesting a higher credit limit. You want to pay early in the billing cycle to make sure you do not wind up with a late fee. Requesting a modestly higher limit may be okay if you have been living comfortably within your budget for some time, but you should make sure you aren't just looking for a way to get quick gratification from impulse shopping when you would be better off building wealth.
- Hiding purchases from your family, or fighting with your spouse about how to deal with your financial situation. Financial problems and domestic problems often go hand-in-hand. The household budget must be a family decision, and you must stick to that budget once it is set.
- Depending on parents and friends to bail you out of financial squeezes.

CHAPTER SEVEN

Credit Reports and Credit Scores

In Chapter Eight we will look at how to rebuild your credit, but first you should understand how lenders decide whether or not to offer credit and on what terms they will offer it. You should also understand some of the tools you can use to affect your credit score.

Remember, lenders are in business to make a profit. They lend you money and collect interest on the loans. To do this successfully, they have to minimize their risks by limiting the number of "bad loans" that don't get repaid. When you apply for a loan, lenders examine your credit history and assess the risk that you won't repay the loan. Borrowers with the best credit records, higher incomes, and job stability tend to get the best terms because they are less likely to default on the loan. Higher risk borrowers will typically be charged higher interest rates or fees. And, if your credit record suggests too much risk, lenders may simply refuse to offer credit.

What Is Your Credit Report?

Your credit report is a compilation of data about you that has been gathered by credit reporting agencies or "credit bureaus." The credit reporting agencies sell this information to lenders and other companies and organizations with a legitimate business need to know how you manage credit. How you handle credit today will affect your access to credit later, because lenders review your credit history when deciding whether to lend you money.

The information included in your credit report includes:

- **Identifying information** — including Social Security number, address and date of birth. This information is used to ensure that the credit report information is accurate and matched with the right person. It can also help detect and prevent identity fraud.
- **Employment history** — where you've worked and for how long.
- **Credit history** — account records with creditors.
- **Inquiries** — a list of who has requested your credit report.
- **Public records** — including collections accounts, bankruptcies, and late child support payments.

Most lenders use a mathematical formula to generate a "score" to help them determine if you are a good credit risk. This is called a "credit score" and the most frequently used version is the FICO score created by Fair Isaac and Company. A FICO score is a snapshot of your credit risk picture at a particular point in time. FICO scores range between 300 and 850 with higher values indicating a lower risk to lenders.

As you can see in Figure 6.1, your credit score is determined by five factors: payment history, outstanding debt, length of credit history, recent inquiries, and types of credit in use. Each of these factors is weighted differently to determine your score:

Figure 6.1. What Is In a Credit Score?

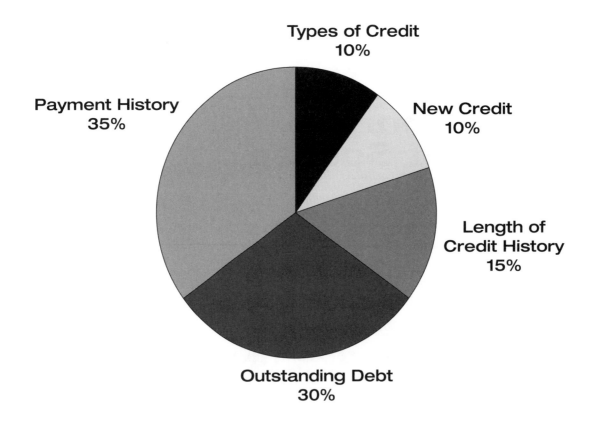

Types of Credit
10%

New Credit
10%

Length of
Credit History
15%

Payment History
35%

Outstanding Debt
30%

- **Payment History (35%)** — late payments, judgments, bankruptcy, and tax liens can lower your score.
- **Outstanding Debt (30%)** — maxing out your credit cards can lower your score.
- **Length of Credit History (15%)** — long relationships with banks and credit unions have a positive influence on your score.
- **Recent Inquiries (10%)** — too many inquiries in response to applications for credit within a short period of time can lower your score because it suggests you are frantic for credit and/or may soon be overexposed.
- **Types of Credit in Use (10%)** — too many open lines of credit (i.e. credit cards, retail accounts, installment loans, mortgage accounts) can lower your score. Loans from finance companies generally lower your score, especially when there are no other types of credit reported.

Get a Free Copy of Your Credit Report

A recent amendment to the federal Fair Credit Reporting Act (FCRA) requires each of the nationwide consumer reporting companies to provide you with a free copy of your credit report, at your request, once every 12 months, from each of the three major credit bureaus. A credit report reflects the history of your borrowing and payment practices for a seven-to-ten-year period.

To order your free credit report,

- Click on www.annualcreditreport.com, or
- Call 877-322-8228, or
- Send a request to:
  Annual Credit Report Request Service
  P.O. Box 105281
  Atlanta, GA 30348-5281

If you request your report online, you should be able to access it immediately. If you order it over the phone or through the mail, it will be processed and mailed to you within 15 days. Or, you may contact the credit bureaus directly to get your report.

Make sure you review all three of your credit bureau reports because there may be some differences among them. Your creditors do not necessarily report information to all three credit bureaus, and they do not always share information. It might be wise to request copies a few months after your bankruptcy has been filed to get an idea of the impact the bankruptcy had on your credit rating.

Review Your Credit Report

If you have questions about how to read your credit report, you should contact the three national credit bureaus at:

- **Equifax**
  1-800-685-1111; www.equifax.com
- **Experian**
  1-888-397-3742; www.experian.com
- **TransUnion**
  1-800-888-4213; www.transunion.com

Correct Mistakes on Your Credit Report

When you receive your report, check for any negative information. There are maximum periods of times that negative information may stay on your record. They are:

- **Civil Judgments**
  Seven years from the date they were filed
- **Tax Liens**
  Seven years from when you paid them
- **Chapter 7 Bankruptcy**
  10 years after discharge
- **Chapter 13 Bankruptcy**
  10 years after discharge

If the appropriate amount of time has passed and the information is still in your report, call and follow up with a letter asking that the negative information be removed.

If you find errors on your credit report, you will need to file a dispute with the credit bureau. This can be processed online or by sending a letter to the credit bureau. Once the credit bureau has received your letter of dispute, it will contact the creditor that has listed the item on your report. The creditor will have 30 days to verify the information. If it cannot verify the listing or cannot meet the time limit, the bureau is required to remove the disputed listing from your report. Even if negative information is correct, send a letter to the credit bureau explaining the circumstances if you feel that might help. At least the credit bureau will have the letter on file for future reference.

Why Is My FICO (Credit) Score So Important?

The interest rates you are charged on loans may be determined by your FICO score. The higher your score, the better chance you have of getting a better rate. FICO scores can also be used to determine your homeowner and auto insurance premiums and whether or not you qualify for a loan.

Laws to Help You

The Equal Credit Opportunity Act (ECOA) protects you against discrimination by creditors (banks, loan and finance companies, department stores) based on race, sex, age, martial status, national origin, or because you receive public assistance. It ensures that all consumers are given an equal chance to obtain credit. It does *not* mean that everyone who applies for credit will get it, but that only reasonable factors are used to determine creditworthiness (such as income, expenses, credit history and debt). For a detailed list of rules creditors must follow when offering credit to consumers, go to the Federal Trade Commission Web site at www.ftc.gov.

The Consumer Protection Act of 1968 and the Truth and Lending disclosures which are based on that law require creditors to state the cost of borrowing in a common language so the consumer can determine the true costs of any loan. It allows you to shop and compare for a loan and helps you get the best deal. For more information on the protections afforded you under the Act, go to www.federalreserve.gov.

CHAPTER EIGHT

Rebuilding Your Credit

Developing Good Credit Habits

Whatever your personal financial situation, this chapter will outline successful strategies for rebuilding your credit. This is possible even though you've filed for bankruptcy. The chapter will also provide helpful information about shopping around for credit and managing credit card accounts once you re-enter the credit marketplace.

So what do you need to do to re-establish your credit? Here are some good credit habits that can help.

Manage Your Credit Card(s) Well

This is a big one and includes many important items:

- Check your credit report, as discussed in the previous chapter. Make sure that there are no errors on your report, and, if there are, report them immediately. Also check for missing information on accounts that are current because this information can boost your FICO score. Make sure that your credit report is accurate regarding your employment, current residence, and personal contact information. It does not have to include this information, but often will.

- If you still have open credit card accounts after bankruptcy, keep at least one of them open (preferably an older credit card account). Consumers who use credit accounts moderately—charging low balances and repaying on time—are considered a better risk than those who do not use credit at all.

- Since you have declared bankruptcy, it is likely that most of your credit card accounts were closed. If this is the case, do not rush to apply for new cards. While it will help your FICO score to have a credit payment history, it will not help you to apply for a credit card before you are financially ready. Make sure that you are able to stick to your budget and start off small, perhaps with a gas station or department store card that you use for small purchases each month and pay off in full.

- You might find that you cannot get a traditional credit card account on your own; you need a co-signer or must apply for a *secured* credit card. A secured credit card requires you to deposit money into an account as collateral. Your line of credit is determined by the amount of your deposit. In effect, this is a convenience card that enables you to more easily conduct transactions without carrying a large amount of cash. Unlike a traditional card, a secured card does not provide access to additional credit.

Pay Bills on Time

This goes with sticking to your budget—you should pay all of your bills on time to avoid late fees or increases in your interest rates from missed payments. This includes credit card payments, debts that you reaffirmed in bankruptcy, utilities, car loans, and rent or mortgage payments. Remember, all lenders will be looking at your payment habits to determine if you are practicing good financial behavior following your bankruptcy.

Some people find it helpful to keep track of when specific bills are due on a calendar. Currently, late fees average around $30. In coming years, many predict late fees will increase. In addition to late fees, credit card issuers can increase your interest rate as a result of late payments. The "universal default" clause found in most credit card agreements also allows the credit card issuer to increase your interest rate on its card if you default on another account. This is just another reason to stay on top of all of your bills.

Open a Checking or Savings Account

Checking and savings accounts signal that you are able to use money wisely, and they may be used as collateral when applying for secured credit cards or small loans. A secured credit card or small loan repaid on time is a plus. As discussed earlier, accumulating funds for unexpected expenses in a checking or savings account makes it less likely you might have to resort to high interest loans or other expensive short-term credit to get you past a cash squeeze. And, as we've said, saving helps you build wealth for the long term. Even when your credit has recovered, you should continue to save or invest at least 10 percent of your pay.

Shop Around for a Credit Card

Why is it that people will shop around for months to find the best deal on a television set, but never read the fine print on a credit card offer? Most people assume that the costs associated with all credit cards are the same because they are identical products. While the products are, in fact, the same, the terms on which those products are offered to consumers are often very different. Because they compete for your business, credit card companies offer a range of different policies on late fees, inter-

est rates and cardholder services. Before applying for a credit card, you should shop among different providers of credit, reading the fine print before applying. Below are some questions to ask any provider of credit:

- Is there an annual fee for using the card? Transaction fee? Late payment fee? Over-the-limit charge? Balance transfer fee?
- What is the current interest rate (APR)? Is it a fixed fee that stays the same from month to month, or can it move up or down depending on interest rates in the economy or even depending on how you use the card?
- How soon after purchase does the card issuer begin to charge interest? Typically, cards have a "grace period," and if you pay the balance in full during the time, you will not be charged interest. That grace period should be disclosed.
- What is the method for calculating the balances on which you pay interest? That's important because it affects how much you pay. For example, a card may charge interest on an average balance during a certain period. Or, it might charge you on the total balance at the end of a billing period.
- If collateral is necessary, how will it be held?
- Is there a "universal default" clause in the credit card agreement that allows the issuer to raise the interest rate on the card if you default on another account?
- How many days' notice are given to change the terms of credit?
- What other services are offered with the credit card (e.g., rental insurance, extended warranties, fraud or theft protection, rebate programs)?
- What are the policies and procedures for lost/stolen cards, and are you responsible to pay for charges when somebody else illegally uses your card? Under the law, your responsibility is limited to $50 if you report that your card has been lost or stolen. But some credit card companies won't hold you responsible for any liability at all.
- What protection is offered if your identity is stolen and credit is used falsely in that way?

Frequently Asked Questions

- **How many credit cards should I carry?** As we've said previously, your first focus is to get back on your feet and limit your use of credit. That's why we recommend no more than three. No matter how many cards you have, you should keep careful track of your expenditures and try very hard to limit what you charge to an amount you can pay in full every month.

- **How long will it take to rebuild my credit?** Anyone who promises you a quick fix is not being honest. It will usually take about two years for credit to be rebuilt enough that you do not get rejected for a major credit card at reasonable interest rates, and up to four years to qualify for a mortgage with reasonable terms.

- **Should I transfer balances from higher interest credit cards to lower rate cards?** This is a tough one. You should be conservative about transferring balances — even to ones with low or zero interest rates. Every time you transfer your balance, it will show up on your credit report and will signal that you are postponing, rather than paying off, your debt. Think carefully about whether this move is really reducing your debt or just putting it off. If it is just putting it off, then it is generally not a good idea to transfer funds from one account to another.

CHAPTER NINE

Predatory Lending and Identity Theft

A Few Words about Predatory Lending

In years past, an individual who had filed for bankruptcy would have had few, if any, offers of credit. Recently, however, many lenders have developed specialized businesses that seek out and lend to individuals who are emerging from bankruptcy. It is likely that you will begin receiving such offers in the mail or by phone. These offers may sound very much like the offers you received prior to filing for bankruptcy. **They are not!** Typically, they will involve much higher interest rates or other unfavorable terms. They will also come with much stiffer penalties for late payments or if you don't comply with complex loan requirements.

Lending to people with credit problems is a legitimate business. But some of these offers may come from "predatory lenders" who charge high rates and count on you to ultimately default. These predatory lenders then walk away with the profits from your payments and also repossess the items you bought with the loan.

In addition, these loans are particularly risky because of the legal restrictions on how often a person can file a bankruptcy case and receive a discharge. For example, if you receive a Chapter 7 discharge, you are not permitted to receive another Chapter 7 discharge unless the second case is filed more than **eight years after** the first case. (Although they are shorter, time limitations also apply to Chapter 13 cases.)

Once you are back in the market for credit, you should know how to assess these offers. See page 54 for a list of items to watch for when considering an offer of new credit. Most of the items listed are legal but costly. A few, such as providing false information, are clearly wrong. If you believe a potential lender may be engaging in fraudulent or dishonest behavior, report it immediately to your local consumer affairs agency and end your contact with that lender.

Identity Theft

Identity theft is when someone uses your personal information (name, Social Security number, credit card information, etc.) without your consent to commit fraud and/or other crimes. The United States Office of Consumer Affairs reports that it received more than 635,000 consumer fraud and identity theft complaints in 2004. Consumers reported losses from fraud of over $547 million.[6]

How Do Identity Thieves Get Your Personal Information?

- From businesses and other institutions by:
  - Stealing records while on the job
  - Bribing employees who have access to records
  - Hacking records
  - Conning information out of employees
- Stealing mail from your mailbox.
- "Dumpster diving" — rummaging through your trash, the trash of businesses, or public trash dumps.

---

[6]Federal Trade Commission Report, "National and State Trends In Fraud & Identity Theft, January — December 2004, pg. 2.

Warnings Signs of Costly or Potentially Damaging Loans

Fees and Interest Rates

- High interest rates as calculated by the Annual Percentage Rate (APR)
- Unusual variable interest rate terms that can go up significantly on short notice. This includes "teaser" or introductory rates
- High fees and closing costs
- Significant prepayment penalties if you pay off the loan ahead of schedule
- Balloon payments (large amounts over and above your monthly payment at a future date, often to close out the loan)
- Negative amortization (your monthly payment will not keep pace with interest charged, so the amount of money you owe goes up even when you are making all of your required payments)

Other Loan Terms

- Credit insurance required as part of the loan
- Mandatory co-signers

Loan Purpose

- Suggestions by a lender that you refinance a recent loan it made to you. (Referred to as "flipping," the practice of frequent refinancing generates substantial fees for the lender and growing expenses for the borrower.)
- Unnecessary debt consolidation

Documentation and Other Issues

- Post-dating documents
- Large loan broker fees or kickbacks
- Making unaffordable loans based on the value of your property
- Forged signatures
- Inaccurate income listed by the lender on loan applications
- Unrealistic (inflated) appraisals of your home's value
- Terms at closing different from what you were promised
- Rush, rush, rush to close the deal

These are just a few of the more obvious warning signs. When in doubt, ask your certified credit counselor.

- "Phishing" — stealing personal information through an email or phone in which they pose as a legitimate company and claim that you have a problem with your account.
- "Skimming" — stealing credit or debit card numbers by capturing the information in a data storage device that they have attached to an ATM or credit card machine.
- "Shoulder surfing" — looking over your shoulder for passwords and PIN numbers at ATM machines and stores.

What Can Identity Thieves Do With Your Personal Information?

- They may open new credit card accounts in your name.
- They may change the address on your existing credit card accounts.
- They may open a bank account in your name and write bad checks on that account.
- They may file for bankruptcy under your name.
- They may take out a mortgage, auto loans, or establish phone or wireless service in your name.
- They may get a job or file fraudulent tax returns in your name.
- They may give your name to the police during an arrest. If they don't show up for their court date, a warrant for their arrest is issued in your name.

What Do You Do If You Think Your Identity Has Been Stolen?

- Contact the fraud departments of any one of the three major credit bureaus to place a fraud alert on your credit file. This is especially critical since your credit report has already suffered damage as a result of your bankruptcy. The fraud alert asks creditors to contact you before opening any new accounts or making changes to your existing accounts. As soon as one of the credit bureaus confirms your fraud alert, the other two credit bureaus will be automatically notified to place fraud alerts on your accounts as well. Credit reports from

all three bureaus will be sent to you free of charge.
  – Equifax
    www.equifax.com or 1-800-525-6285
  – Experian
    www.experian.com or 1-800-397-3742
  – TransUnion
    www.transunion.com or 1-800-680-7289
- Close the accounts that you know or believe to have been tampered with or opened fraudulently.
- File a police report. Get a copy of the report to submit to your creditors and others who may require proof of the crime.
- File a complaint with the Federal Trade Commission (FTC). The FTC maintains a database of identity theft cases. That database is used to learn more about identity theft and how to prevent future cases. It is also used by law enforcement agencies for investigations. FTC 1-877-438-4338 or www.consumer.gov/idtheft
- Consult an attorney to determine legal action to take against creditors and/or credit bureaus if they are not cooperative in removing fraudulent entries from your credit report.
- Contact the local Office of the United States Trustee if a bankruptcy case has been filed fraudulently in your name.

How Do You Prevent Identity Theft?

No one can fully prevent identity theft, but there are steps you can take to reduce your chances of becoming a victim:

Steps to Reduce the Chance of Identity Theft

- Place passwords on your online credit card, bank, and phone accounts. Avoid using easily available information like your birth date, phone number, or mother's maiden name.
- Sign your credit or debit cards as soon as they arrive.
- Carry your cards in a safe place separate from your wallet.

- Do not carry your Social Security Card; keep it in a secure place.
- Keep a record of your account numbers, their expiration dates, and the phone number and address of each company in a secure place.
- Never give out personal or account information in response to an email query unless it is part of a transaction that you initiated.
- Save receipts to compare with billing statements.
- Open bills promptly and reconcile accounts monthly.
- Treat your mail and trash carefully.
  - Deposit outgoing mail in secured mailboxes such as a U.S. Post Office box.
  - If you are planning to be away from home and unable to pick up your mail, have the Postal Service hold your mail until you are able to pick it up.
    - Tear or shred charge receipts, copies of credit applications, bank statements, and other documents with your personal information.
    - Be cautious about using a personal computer to store personal information.
    - Update virus protection software regularly.
    - Do not open files sent to you by strangers.
    - Use a firewall program.
    - Use a secure browser.
    - Avoid storing personal information on a laptop.
    - Before disposing of a computer, delete all personal information from the hard drive.
- If your credit and debit cards are lost or stolen, immediately contact the issuers of the cards.
- Consider purchasing a service that alerts you to any request for your credit information or unusual activity on your account.

CHAPTER TEN

What is Insurance For?

Protecting Yourself from Financial Losses

All choices involve risk. For example, driving a car involves the risk of an accident. You can reduce that risk by limiting the amount of time you drive your car, walking, or by taking public transportation whenever possible. Or, you might take a defensive driving course to enhance your chances of avoiding accidents caused by somebody else's mistakes.

Similarly, insurance is about reducing financial risk. Auto insurance won't reduce your chances of being involved in an accident, but it will protect you from financial loss due to the car repairs, medical costs, or lawsuits that result from an accident. Buying health insurance reduces the risk that medical bills from a serious illness or injury will wipe out your savings or push you into deep debt. Homeowner's insurance won't prevent a fire, but it means you will likely be able to afford a new place to live if your home burns down.

Protecting yourself against sudden financial catastrophe is as much a part of good money management as paying your bills and accumulating wealth. Often, people look only at the cost of buying insurance and decide not to buy it because they don't receive anything tangible in return. But that's like saying seat belts are useless because they don't matter unless you become involved in an accident.

Having just gone through bankruptcy, you will have to work hard to rebuild your financial well-being. Does it really make sense to jeopardize all that hard work by refusing to pay insurance premiums? Real financial wellness means protecting yourself against the financial impact of events such as illness or accidents that you can't control.

You may not be able to afford all of the insurance that you would like. You will have to make choices. For this reason, it is important to understand the types of insurance protections available, the cost of such insurance, and the ways to decide how much insurance is needed. This knowledge will enable you to make informed decisions.

When choosing insurance coverage, the best rule is to *"insure only what you cannot afford to lose."* In other words, if the loss would create a crippling economic burden and cause you major financial harm, then you should have insurance for that loss. This will create monthly or periodic expenses for the insurance, so make sure you include the cost in your budget. Paying for any type of insurance in the aftermath of a bankruptcy may be difficult, but not having insurance can lead to an even worse financial outcome. In fact, it's possible that inadequate insurance coverage contributed to your bankruptcy. Part of the process of rebuilding your financial life involves spending a relatively small amount each month to protect yourself from a catastrophic loss. That's what insurance is for. But you also want to avoid buying more insurance than you need.

Types of Insurance

Type	Purpose	Examples of Coverage
Automobile	• Provides financial protection from losses due to an auto accident or other damage to a car. • Most states require licensed drivers to have automobile insurance.	• **Collision:** Provides for the repair or replacement of the policy owner's car damaged in an accident. • **Liability:** Covers the cost of property damage or injuries to others caused by the policy owner. • **Comprehensive:** Covers the cost of damage to an auto as a result of fire, theft, or natural disaster.
Health	• Provides payment of certain health care costs.	• **Basic:** Covers office visits, laboratory, hospital costs, and routine care. • **Major Medical:** Protects against large bills caused by catastrophic illness or injury. • **Dental and Vision:** Covers some of the cost of routine exams and specific services.
Renter's	• Provides financial protection in case of loss of personal possessions in a rental unit.	• Reimburses policy owner for loss of possessions in a rental unit due to fire, theft, water damage, etc.
Homeowner's	• Protects against financial loss from damage to your home or its contents, as well as injury to others on the property. • Most financial institutions require homeowner's insurance for mortgages.	• **Physical Damage:** Reimburses for fire or water damage to house or other structures on the property. • **Loss or Theft:** Reimburses for personal property damaged or stolen. • **Liability:** Protects against loss from a lawsuit for injuries to people on your property.
Life	• Provides financial protection to the dependents of the policy owner when the policy owner dies.	• **Term Life:** Offers protection for a specified period of time. • **Whole Life:** Offers protection that remains in effect during the lifetime of the insured and acquires a cash value.
Disability	• Provides income over a specified period when a person is ill or unable to work.	Policy owner selects a replacement income for lost wages if an illness or accident prevents the person from working.
Long-Term Care	• Pays for the daily care of the elderly or permanently ill. Care can range from occasional home visits to assisted living to full-time nursing care.	Policy owner determines a daily benefit amount and benefit duration. Additional features such as inflation protection can be added to the policy.

Costs of Insurance

Generally, you can buy insurance to cover any loss. However, the more insurance you have, the more it costs. Buying insurance is always a trade-off and depends upon how much risk you are willing to assume and how much risk you want an insurance company to take on. For example, most life insurance companies offer both term and whole-life insurance. Term insurance will pay your survivors an amount of money if you die within the term of the policy—20 years, for example. Normally, if you are young, this type of insurance will not cost very much. That's because the likelihood of dying young is very small and the risk to the insurance company is very low.

As you get older, the cost of term life insurance goes up dramatically to offset the increasing likelihood that you will die during the term of the policy and the insurance company will have to pay a death benefit. When the agreed period of coverage runs out, the insurance company may decide not to offer you new insurance, especially if your health has declined. Or, it may do so only at a price that many people will not be able to afford. In essence, with term insurance the insurance company is very happy to accept the risk of your death when you are young but much less eager to accept the risk when you get older. You pay very little in the early years, but you run the risk of not being able to obtain affordable life insurance as you get older.

With whole life insurance, the insurance company agrees from the outset that it will insure you for as long as you are willing to pay the premiums. Because it is accepting a much longer-term risk, the insurance company charges you a much higher cost than with term insurance in the early years. But the monthly cost of whole life insurance stays the same throughout your life. The benefit of pay-ing more in the early years is that you will always have life insurance even if your health deteriorates and it will not get more expensive in your later years.

Whole life insurance also builds cash value upon which you can draw. Over time, the cash value may be greater than what you've paid for the insurance. **No matter what your age, if you are the primary or sole wage earner, you should try to buy enough life insurance to ensure the financial well-being of your family until other family members can earn an adequate income.**

Buying health insurance involves different considerations than life insurance. One way to decide how much insurance you need is to determine how much you could afford to pay out of your own pocket. Can you afford a $5,000 medical bill? If you can, then it makes sense to buy health insurance with a $5,000 catastrophic cap. This means that, no matter how high the medical bills, you will only have to pay $5,000 for your medical care. The higher the cap and the deductibles (the amount you pay from your own pocket before the insurance kicks in), the lower your monthly premiums. The lower the cap, the more you will pay each month. If you and your family are in generally good health, higher deductibles and lower premiums are often the best way to go. In most years, you will probably not pay the full amount of deductibles and your out-of-pocket payments will be less than what you save in premiums.

This same type of approach applies to other types of insurance. The key is to decide how much you can afford to pay for the loss and how much you want the insurance company to pay. Generally, you should have the highest deductible you can afford to pay in the event of a loss because this keeps your fixed insurance expenses as low as possible.

CHAPTER ELEVEN

Financial Tools and Resources

There are many sources to help you in your search for personal finance information. First of all, why not check your local newspaper? Almost every newspaper has at least one column dealing with personal finance issues. They often appear in the Sunday edition. Some columnists address issues currently in the news. They often recommend books that will provide readers with further information.

Most state and local governments have an office that deals with consumer issues. It is usually called the Division of Consumer Affairs. In addition, most State Attorney General Offices deal with consumer issues. Some will mediate problems for consumers and even publish material dealing with many consumer issues.

Many books have been written on the subject of personal finance. Listed below are several, along with a short synopsis of the content of each.

50 Simple Things You Can Do to Improve Your Personal Finances, Ilyce R. Glink, Three Rivers Press, 2001.
This book covers a broad range of topics: paperwork organization, budgets, credit, investing, insurance, taxes and retirement planning. Ms. Glink has also published 100 Questions Every First-Time Home Buyer Should Ask, and *100 Questions You Should Ask About Your Personal Finances.*

Wealth Happens One Day at a Time, Brooke M. Stephens, Harper Business, 2000.
In a series of 365 readings, Ms. Stephens deals with the role of money in our lives, budgeting, credit and debt, long-term asset accumulation, insurance, and finally, retirement and estate planning.

Don't Spend Your Raise, Dara Duguay, McGraw-Hill, 2002.
This book has a total of 60 short readings that fall into the following categories: "Investing in Your Future," "Dollars and Sense," "Livin' Large, Credit: It's Not Your Money," "Till Debt Do Us Part," and "The Rainy Day: Finding Your Umbrella."

Pay It Down!, Jean Chatzky, Portfolio, 2004.
The subtitle, From Debt to Wealth on $10 a Day, neatly summarizes the content of this book. The contents are divided into 11 Steps beginning with "Assess the Problem" and ending with "Staying Ahead of the Game." Two excellent parts of the book deal with understanding your FICO score and looking through your budget to "find" money, not a thousand dollars in one place but $10 here and $10 there. Ms. Chatzky, who appears on the *Today Show,* has also written *You Don't Have to Be Rich.*

Take Control of Your Student Loan Debt,
Robin Leonard & Deanne Loonin, 2001.
Today, virtually everyone graduates from college
with student loan debt. This book focuses on helping you get organized to deal with that debt. In
the Appendix you will find the forms to help you
with everything from keeping a telephone log of
calls you make about your loans, to setting up a
monthly budget. State by state information for
consequences of not paying your loans, state
departments of higher education, and state tuition
recovery programs also are provided.

Debt Proof Living, Mary Hunt, Broadman &
Holman, 1999.
Written from the perspective of someone who was
at one time very far in debt and has managed to
repay all of the money and gone on to prosper.
Ms. Hunt offers ways to organize your finances to
deal with any situation.

Think $ingle!, Janet Bodnar, Kiplinger Books,
2003.
Women have traditionally been at a disadvantage
financially. In addition to general financial information, this book addresses issues of interest to
women such as dealing with finances within a
marriage, documents you need to have in place,
investing, divorce, dealing with aging parents, and
carrying on in widowhood. Although this books
deals with many women's issues, the information is
useful to everyone regardless of age or sex.

7 Money Mantras for a Richer Life, Michelle
Singletary, Random House, 2004.
Drawing on her experiences with her grand-
mother, Big Mama, Ms. Singletary neatly divides
money management into seven statements. The
statements, listed in Part One, offer insight into
attitudes toward money and its role in our lives.
Part Two deals with saving, spending, and investing.

**The Total Money Makeover: A Proven Plan
for Financial Fitness,** Dave Ramsey, 2003.
A guide to getting your budget into shape by
helping you pay off your debt. It also can enable
you to recognize the most dangerous money myths
and get you started on building your savings.

How to Ruin Your Financial Life, Ben Stein,
Hay House, 2004.
Many books have been written about the "right
ways to deal with money," and there are still
countless numbers of people declaring bankruptcy.
Mr. Stein takes the contrarian approach by describ-
ing the many ways to ruin yourself financially.
Examples of chapter titles are: "Forget About
Tomorrow," "Compete With Your Friends to See
Who Can Spend the Most," "Don't Balance Your
Checkbook or Keep Track of Your Spending," and
"Get Separated and Divorced Frequently." These
readings are relatively short and humorous and
manage to teach financial lessons.

Surviving Debt, A Guide for Consumers,
The National Consumer Law Center, 2005.

The Richest Man in Babylon, George S.
Clason, Penguin, 1926.
Yes, published first in 1926! These allegorical readings teach such timeless lessons as spend less than
you make, put something aside for a rainy day, and
protect your assets.

Identity Theft Booklet, Federal Reserve Bank
of Boston
Publications and Community Affairs Department
Federal Reserve Bank of Boston
PO Box 55882
Boston, MA 02205

If you have Internet access, there are many excellent sources of information for you. We have
compiled the following a list of some of them.

Federal Reserve Banks

Building Wealth: A Beginner's Guide to Securing Your Financial Future
www.dallasfed.org

Identity Theft and links to a variety of sites
www.bos.frb.org

Bank Products — What is FDIC Protected and What is Not
www.minneapolisfed.org
Search in Consumer Information

Checking
www.frbatlanta.org
Click on Consumer Information
Click on Personal Finance Education
Click on Checkbooklet

Consumer Education Pamphlets on a Variety of Subjects
www.phil.frb.org
www.ftc.gov

Credit Cards, Home Mortgages and Vehicle Leasing Information
www.richmondfed.org
Click on Educational Info
Click on Consumer Information
You can link to the Board of Governors site that has information on these topics.

Free credit reports
www.annualcreditreport.com
877-322-8228

Other Sites Grouped by Topic

General
National Consumer Law Center
www.consumerlaw.org

Social Security Administration
www.ssa.gov
Links to help you find out information about programs associated with the Social Security Administration and to help you print out forms.

Budgeting
Stop Buying Expensive Coffee and Save Calculator
www.hughchou.org/calc/coffee.cgi

Saving
American Savings Education Council
www.asec.org
This site contains brochures you can download as well as a calculator to help you decide how much you need to be saving to reach a specific goal.

Debt
Debt Advice
www.debtadvice.org

American Bankers Association
www.aba.com
Many credit links

Frontline
www.pbs.org
Click on Frontline.
Click on The Secret Life of Credit Cards.
This site contains a credit card quiz, an explanation of credit card terms and a calculator to determine the length of time it will take to pay off charges given a specific rate of interest. **It assumes you are making the minimum monthly payment and will charge no more.**

Stop Mortgage Fraud
www.stopmortgagefraud.com
Stopping abusive lending practices

Identity Theft
Better Business Bureau
www.bbb.org
Click to take an Identity Theft Quiz. Your score will contain tips on ways to make yourself safer from identity theft.

Federal Trade Commission
www.ftc.gov

American Bankers Association
www.aba.com
Phishing

Federal Reserve Bank of Boston
www.bos.frb.org

Executive Office of the United States Trustee Program
www.usdoj.gov/ust

Important telephone numbers for the three major credit reporting companies:

- Equifax   1-800-685-1111; **www.equifax.com**
- Experian   1-888-397-3742; **www.experian.com**
- TransUnion 1-800-888-4213; **www.transunion.com**

No portion of this text is in any way intended as legal advice. Readers are strongly advised to consult an attorney regarding specific bankruptcy issues and questions.

The Decision-Making Matrix

Problem:

	Factors		
Alternatives/Choices			

Your Decision:

Glossary

Asset: Something of value that you possess and that can be valued in cash.

APR: Annual percentage rate. This is the interest percentage you are charged each year to borrow money.

Bankruptcy: A legal proceeding filed in the United States Bankruptcy Court (a federal, not a state court) that permits a person to obtain a *discharge* of his or her obligation to pay certain debts. The bankruptcy laws are intended to allow an honest, but unfortunate *debtor* to obtain a "fresh start." The *debtor* in a Chapter 7 case must surrender any *asset* that is not *exempt property* to a *bankruptcy trustee,* who liquidates the *non-exempt property* in order to make payments to *creditors*.

Bankruptcy petition: A legal pleading filed in the United States Bankruptcy Court in which a *debtor* declares *bankruptcy* and sets in motion the legal proceedings necessary to obtain a *discharge* of debts. The *bankruptcy petition* is accompanied by a number of other papers and schedules submitted under penalty of perjury in which the *debtor* makes a full public disclosure of all the *debtor's* debts and *assets*.

Bankruptcy trustee: The person who has been appointed by the United States Trustee (a representative of the United States Department of Justice) to take control of the *debtor's non-exempt property* during the course of the *bankruptcy* proceedings. Protecting the interests of the *creditors* is the *bankruptcy trustee's* responsibility.

Chapter 7 Bankruptcy: A *Chapter 7 bankruptcy* is a case in which a *bankruptcy trustee* is appointed to liquidate any *assets* of the *debtor* that are not *exempt property* for the purpose of making payments to *creditors*. For that reason, a Chapter 7 case is often referred to as a "straight bankruptcy" or a "liquidation case."

Chapter 13 Bankruptcy: A *Chapter 13 bankruptcy* is a case in which the *debtor* with regular income proposes a plan to repay some or all debt over three to five years. For that reason, a Chapter 13 case is sometimes referred to as a "wage earner plan." The Chapter 13 trustee does not take possession of the *debtor's non-exempt property*, but supervises the case and administers the payments to *creditors* under the Chapter 13 plan.

Collateral: Properties or *assets* that are offered to secure a loan or other credit. Collateral becomes subject to seizure on default. For example, if you borrow money to buy a home, that home is "collateral" for the *mortgage* (loan). If you don't make your payments, the lender (mortgagee) can sell your home and use the proceeds to repay the loan.

Creditor: A person or organization to whom you legally owe money as the result of borrowing money from them or entering into other legally enforceable obligations.

Debt Management Plan (DMP):[7] A DMP is a systematic way to pay down your outstanding debt through monthly deposits to an agency, which then distributes these funds to your *creditors*. By participating in this program, you may benefit from reduced or waived finance charges and fewer collection calls.

Debtor: A person who legally owes money to someone or some entity.

Deductions: Any money taken out of your income before you receive it. These can be mandatory, such as federal or state withholding taxes, Social Security, Medicare, child support or spousal maintenance (alimony), or voluntary, such as retirement contributions, union dues, savings deposits, or investments.

Deductible: The amount you have to pay for a loss before your insurance company pays the remaining amount of the loss.

Discharge: A court order that precludes a *creditor* from taking any action to collect a debt. A debtor does not need to repay a debt that has been discharged. Some debts (known as "non-dischargeable debts"), however, are not discharged and must be paid after the *bankruptcy*.

Exempt Property: In a *Chapter 7 bankruptcy*, exempt property is the *debtor's* property protected by law that cannot be seized or liquidated to pay back debt; *non-exempt property* can be liquidated by the Chapter 7 trustee. Depending upon the state in which you file and the circumstances of your case, you may have the option to claim exemptions under federal or state laws, or may be restricted to the exemption laws of a particular state. The Chapter 7 trustee and *creditors* have the right to object to the *debtor's* claim of exempt property. If there is an objection, the validity of the claim of exemption is decided by the Bankruptcy Judge.

Fixed Monthly Expenses: Expenses that are approximately the same every month and that are fairly predictable. These would include *mortgage* or rent payments, utility payments, loan payments, etc.

Foreclosure: When the bank sells your home because you failed to make your *mortgage* payments on time.

Garnishment: When the government or a judgment *creditor* takes money out of your paycheck before you are paid to pay back a debt you owe or some other type of legal obligation (such as court-ordered child support). Your employer must honor the garnishment and send a check directly to the government or *creditor* before paying you the remainder of your wages.

Gross Income: Your total income, either weekly, monthly, or annually. This is the total amount of your income before any *deductions* are taken out.

Gross value: The total, positive value of something before you reduce it by an amount owed on that item.

Home equity: This is the difference between how much your home is worth on the market and how much you owe to a lender. If you have a $100,000 *mortgage*, and your home is worth $200,000, then you have $100,000 in equity. If you sold your home, you would receive $200,000, pay back the lender the $100,000 you owe, and keep $100,000 in profit—your equity. It is one of your *assets*.

Home equity loan: A loan whereby a consumer borrows money and uses the *collateral* in their home to secure a second mortgage on their home. The loan is based on the difference between the amount the homeowner has paid off on the first mortgage and the home's current market value. Like the first mortgage, a default on the loan can enable a lender to foreclose on the home (after the first lender receives any owed amount).

[7]www.nfcc.org

Home equity line of credit: A home equity line of credit is a type of home equity loan in the form of revolving credit in which your home serves as *collateral*. With a home equity line, the lender will approve a specific amount of credit. This is your credit limit, and it is the maximum amount you may borrow at any one time under the plan. Interest rates are usually variable, interest is usually tax deductible, and your monthly payments usually vary depending upon how much of your credit line you have borrowed and what the current interest rate is. There may also be significant penalties if you close the credit line in less than one or two years.

Individual Retirement Account (IRA):[8] Every taxpayer in the United States can start an IRA. An IRA is a retirement investing tool. There are several types of IRAs: Traditional IRAs, Roth IRAs, SIMPLE IRAs, and SEP IRAs. Many types of accounts can be designated as IRAs, including savings accounts, mutual funds, certificates of deposit, money market funds, and others. Depending on the type of IRA, taxes are either deferred or reduced on all the money earned in those accounts. This offers a major tax benefit to the individual for retirement.

Levy:[9] To take property upon a court ordered writ of execution to pay a money judgment that was granted in a lawsuit. A sheriff or other official makes the levy at the judgment holder's request. The property will then be sold at a sheriff's sale in order to provide the money to satisfy the unpaid judgment.

Liability: A debt you owe or any other financial obligation.

Liquidity: The ease with which something can be converted into cash. Cash, by definition, is perfectly liquid. Checks, debit cards, and bank drafts are also fully liquid since they access cash almost immediately. A home is not liquid. The process of converting a home to cash normally takes several weeks or months.

Means Test: If you are filing for a *Chapter 7 bankruptcy*, this is a test your attorney will apply to your situation to determine if you qualify or if you must file under Chapter 13. The means test was adopted by Congress in the Bankruptcy Abuse Prevention and Consumer Protection Act of 2005 and is intended to measure your ability to pay back a portion of your debts.

Median Income: The median is the middle of a distribution: half the scores are above the median and half are below the median. Therefore, a median income is the income among a certain population which lies at the halfway point of all the incomes in that population.

Net Income: Your weekly, monthly or annual income after *deductions* are taken out.

Net value: The *gross value* minus any amount owed on that item. The net value of your car is the "blue book" value of that car minus the amount of any loans on the car.

Non-exempt property: Property you own that can legally be sold by the *bankruptcy trustee* to obtain cash to help repay your debts. See also *exempt property*.

Periodic Expenses: Non-monthly expenses that occur at varying times and in varying amounts throughout the year. These might include car repairs, medical bills, college tuition payments, etc. You should figure out a monthly amount to save for these periodic expenses.

---

[8]www.Investopedia.com
[9]www.legal-explanations.com

Predatory Lending:[10] In the strictest and legal sense of the word, predatory lending refers to secured loans such as home or car loans that are made by the lender with the intention that the borrower can't really pay them, the lender can seize the car or home and sell it for a profit. The word has been expanded to refer to the practice of convincing borrowers to agree to unfair and abusive loan terms. This could be done either through outright deception or through aggressive sales tactics, taking advantage of borrowers' lack of understanding of extremely complicated transactions. Predatory loans for the purchase of a home, for instance, could lead to foreclosure.

Priority Debt:[11] The right to be first, or to be ahead of others' rights or claims. In *bankruptcy* law, taxing authorities, judgment holders, secured *creditors*, *bankruptcy trustees* and attorneys and certain other creditors have the right to be paid before other *creditors*, who are known as the "general unsecured *creditors*."

Reaffirmation:[12] A reaffirmation is a voluntary agreement, between a *debtor* and a *creditor*, that the *debtor* will pay all or a portion of an otherwise *dischargeable* debt after the *debtor* has filed *bankruptcy*. To be valid, the agreement must be made before a *discharge* is granted and must satisfy a number of other technical and disclosure requirements. Unless the reaffirmation agreement is supported by an affidavit from your attorney, it must be approved by the Bankruptcy Judge. The *debtor* has the right to rescind a reaffirmation agreement any time prior to *discharge* or within 60 days after it is filed with the Court (whichever is later).

Secured debt: Debt backed or secured by *collateral* to reduce the risk associated with lending. An example would be a mortgage; your house is considered *collateral* toward the debt. If you default on repayment, the bank seizes your house, sells it, and uses the proceeds to pay back the debt. Nearly all mortgages and *home equity loans* are secured loans using your home as *collateral*.

Universal default:[13] Universal default allows other credit card issuers to raise the cardholder's interest rates on other accounts, even if those other accounts are not in default.

Unsecured debts: Debts with no *collateral*. A *creditor* has no legal right to take your property if it is not specifically listed as *collateral* on a loan. Credit card debt is generally unsecured debt.

Variable Expenses: Monthly expenses over which you exercise the greatest control and to vary based upon your behavior. Entertainment expenses, dues, subscriptions, etc. fall into this category.

Vested: This normally applies to an amount in a company retirement plan that is yours permanently even if you leave the company. If you are not yet "vested," and you leave the company, the non-vested funds are returned to the company.

---

[10]www.investordictionary.com

[11]www.legal-explanations.com

[12]www.encyclopediaofcredit.com

[13]www.answers.com

Appendix — Tables

Table 1: Assets

Assets	Value
Cash and Cash Equivalents	
Checking #1	
Checking #2	
Savings #1	
Savings #2	
Certificates of Deposit	
Other	
Investments (non-retirement)	
Mutual Funds (total)	
Stocks (total)	
Bonds (total)	
Savings Bonds (total)	
Retirement Funds	
IRAs (total)	
401(k) (total)	
403(b) (total)	
SEP/SIMPLE (total)	
Company Retirement Plans (vested)	
Real Property	
Home (current market value)	
Land	
Auto #1 (current market value)	
Auto #2 (current market value)	
Motorcycle	
RV/Plane/ATV	
Other	
Household Goods	
Furniture	
Jewelry	
Computers	
Home Entertainment Center	
Tools	
Valuable Collections	
Total Assets	

Table 2: Liabilities

Liabilities	Amount Owed
Long-Term Loans	
Mortgage Amount	
Second Mortgage	
Home Equity Line of Credit	
Student Loan #1	
Student Loan #2	
Consolidation Loan	
Other Bank Loans	
Auto Loan #1	
Auto Loan #2	
Credit Cards	
MasterCard #1	
MasterCard #2	
Discover Card #1	
Discover Card #2	
Visa #1	
Visa #2	
American Express	
Dept. Store #1	
Dept. Store #2	
Dept. Store #3	
Gas (total)	
Taxes Owed	
Income	
Property	
Tax liens	
Misc. Other Debts	
Relatives	
Friends	
Medical Bills	
Checking Account Overdraft Balances	
Payday Loans	
Total Liabilities	
Calculate Your Net Worth	
Total Assets	
Minus Total Liabilities	
Equals Your Net Worth	

Table 3: Net Monthly Income

Monthly Income Source	Monthly Income		
	Current Monthly Income	Necessary Changes	Planned Net Income
Net Income #1 (income less taxes, Social Security, Medicare)			
Net Income #2 (income less taxes, Social Security, Medicare)			
Net Income #3 (income taxes, Social Security, Medicare)			
Child Support Received			
Spousal Support Received			
Military Retirement			
Other Retirement			
Social Security Received (after taxes)			
Other Income (list source)			
Total Take-Home Income			

Table 4: Daily Expense Tracking Sheet

	Sunday	Monday	Tuesday	Wednesday	Thursday	Friday	Saturday
Income: Date/ Amount/ Source Full Month							
Expenses Item/ Amount Week 1							
Week 2							
Week 3							
Week 4							
Week 5							

Table 5: Monthly Fixed Expenses

Monthly Fixed Expenses	Current Monthly Spending	Necessary Changes	Planned Budget
Mortgage #1			
Mortgage #2			
Auto Loan/Lease # 1			
Auto Loan/Lease # 2			
RV Loan			
Home Equity Loan			
Debt Consolidation/Other Loan(s)			
Student Loan(s)			
Rent			
Condo or Homeowner Association Fees			
Electricity			
Oil or Gas Heat			
Water			
Garbage Collection			
Sewer			
Phone (land line)			
Cell Phones, Pagers, PDA			
Cable/Satellite TV/TiVo Boxes			
Internet Access			
Car Insurance			
Health Insurance (if it isn't deducted from your paycheck)			
Long-Term Care Insurance			
Child Support			
Alimony			
Medical/Dental Payments			
Retirement Savings			
Emergency Fund Savings			
Other:			
Total Monthly Fixed Expenses			

Table 6: Monthly Savings for Periodic Expenses

Monthly Savings for Periodic Expenses (You save a certain amount each month)	Total Annual Amount	Monthly Amount Saved (annual/12)	Necessary Changes	Planned Budget
Property Taxes (if not in your mortgage payment)				
School Taxes (if not in your mortgage payment)				
State and Local Taxes (if not deducted from your paycheck)				
Quarterly Income Taxes				
Insurance (if not monthly)				
Car Registration/License Tag Renewal				
Car Maintenance				
Home Repair				
Water (if not monthly)				
Sewer (if not monthly)				
Garbage (if not monthly)				
Medical (not regular)				
Dental (not regular)				
Veterinarian				
Gifts				
Vacation/Travel				
Tuition and School Costs				
Memberships				
Charitable Donations (one time)				
Other:				
Other:				
Other:				
Other:				
Total Monthly Periodic Expenses				

Table 7: Monthly Variable Expenses

Total Monthly Variable Expenses (Spending you can change)	Current Spending	Necessary Changes	Planned Budget
Card #1			
Card #2			
Card #3			
Card #4			
Card #5			
Store Card(s) (total)			
Gas Card(s) (total)			
Other Credit Lines Not Included in Table #5			
Groceries			
Eating Out (include restaurants, fast food, lunches, etc)			
School Lunches			
Gasoline, Tolls, Parking			
Public Transportation — Bus, Train, Subway			
Health Club Membership			
Daily Coffee/Snacks			
Laundry/Dry Cleaning			
Household Items (not grocery)			
Pet Care and Supplies			
Baby Items			
Children's Allowances			
Hair Cuts/Grooming/Manicures, etc.			
Cosmetics			
Clothes			
Entertainment:			
Movie			
Movie/Game Rental			
Cable On-Demand Movies			
Sports Event: Games, Races			
Concerts			
Play/Dinner Theater			
Symphony			
Day Trips to Amusement Parks			
Other			
CDs			
Club Dues			
Babysitter/Day Care			

(continued next page)

Table 7: Monthly Variable Expenses (continued)

Total Monthly Variable Expenses (Spending you can change)	Current Spending	Necessary Changes	Planned Budget
Lessons: Music/Sports/Tutoring			
Field Trips			
ATM Withdrawals (if you have not already listed elsewhere what you spent the money on)			
ATM Fees			
Computer/Online Expenses			
Donations/Tithe			
Lawn Service			
Occupational Licenses/Fees			
Emergency Savings			
Retirement Savings			
Tobacco/Alcohol			
Magazine Subscriptions			
Misc. Spending Money			
Postage			
Other:			
Other:			
Total Monthly Variable Expenses			

Table 8: Where You Stand

Summing It All Up			
	Current ($)	Necessary Changes ($)	Planned ($)
1. Total Monthly Take-Home Income (from Table 3)			
2. Total Monthly Fixed Expenses (from Table 5)			
3. Subtract Line 2 from Line 1			
4. Total Monthly Savings for Periodic Expenses (from Table 6)			
5. Subtract Line 4 from Line 3			
6. Total Monthly Variable Expenses (from Table 7)			
7. Subtract Line 6 from Line 5			
The amount on line 7 is your **Surplus** if it is **positive** OR your **Shortage** if it is **negative**.			